Handle with Care!

Also by Sinclair B. Ferguson:

The Christian Life

Handle with Care!

A guide to using the Bible

SINCLAIR B. FERGUSON

HODDER AND STOUGHTON
LONDON SYDNEY AUCKLAND TORONTO

All quotations from the Bible are
taken from The New International Version.

British Library Cataloguing in Publication Data
Ferguson, Sinclair B.
  Handle with Care!
  1. Bible—Study
  I. Title
  220'.07   BS600.2
  ISBN 0 340 28197 9

*Printed in Great Britain for Hodder and Stoughton Limited, Mill Road,
Dunton Green, Sevenoaks, Kent by Richard Clay (The Chaucer Press) Ltd.,
Bungay, Suffolk. Typeset by Hewer Text Composition Services.*

Hodder and Stoughton Editorial Office: 47 Bedford Square, London WC1B 3DP.

To
Jim and Mary Melvin

Contents

Introduction

Recently there has been a controversy among scholars and Christian writers. It has come to be known (after the title of the American publication which signalled the first round of the contest) as 'the battle for the Bible'. It is not really a new controversy. Many of its arguments have been heard and used before. But, so far, it is a 'battle' which scholars, rather than ordinary Christians, have waged. It is not the purpose of this book to discuss that battle!

Instead, these pages are written out of the conviction that there is another 'battle for the Bible' being fought. This other battle is fought out day by day in the life of every Christian. It is the battle to read, understand, and put into practice the message of the Bible. In fact, in many ways it is a much wider battle than the other one, because it includes Christians of very many different backgrounds and points of view. It includes you and me. It is certainly an ancient battle.

Some of those who argue about the infallibility of God's word point back to the prototype of their debate, which can be found in the early chapters of the book of Genesis. There, Satan said: 'Surely God did not say that!' 'Surely you don't really believe God's word!'

But the action in that first conflict was not confined to the authority of God's word. In a very subtle way it was also about exactly what it was that God had said, how it should be interpreted ('You will not "die" in that sense,' said Satan), and whether or not it would be obeyed. This is exactly the battle which most of us who are ordinary Christians have to fight day by day. We have to make room in our lives to listen to what God is saying through his word; we do not always find it easy to understand rightly what is written in the Scriptures; we are constantly faced with the challenge of how to apply teaching given to men so long ago to our own situation. And then there is the ultimate issue— how can I follow this teaching in practical obedience in my own life?

This is the battle which, I must confess, I find myself fighting. It is part of the battle of the Christian life in general, and so I expect to keep fighting it to the end of my life. I have not always succeeded in it: indeed, in some ways I find that the fight is tougher as I grow older.

I have been reading the Bible for most of my life now. As a nine-year-old I joined the Scripture Union and began daily to read a portion of God's word, praying that he would open my eyes to discover wonderful things in it. I think I found it easier then to make time, and to take time to read and inwardly digest the message of God's word. I have often thought that I have lived off the capital which I was able to invest then. Now, life is full of duties and responsibilities; time seems to disappear at an alarming speed. Increasingly I find that time has to be 'redeemed' (Eph. 5:16). But that is true of most of us. It is this shared experience which is one of my main motivations for writing this book. I hope that it will not only encourage you to devote time and energy to studying God's word, but will save you going up the many cul-de-sacs into which Bible-readers so often seem to wander.

Alongside the many valuable books which are being written today about the authority and inspiration of the Bible, there is room for another book which is perhaps a little more obviously practical. I believe that for this reason: it is one thing to say that the Bible is God's infallible word; or even that it is God's inerrant word. It is another thing to live in the light of that faith; to understand the Bible properly with our minds and obey it fully in our lives. It is terribly possible to protest loudly about the authority of Scripture, but to live a life and exhibit a spirit which show little of the grace of that Spirit who is the Author of Scripture.

It is possible for two people to agree that Scripture is God's infallible word, and yet, because one (or both) wrongly interpret Scripture, for them practically to be reading two different books. But if we do not rightly handle God's word, rightly understanding and applying it, our profession of its infallibility will be of little real consequence in our lives. It is because the Bible says to us 'Handle me properly', as well as 'Believe me completely', that I have tried to provide an introduction to the study of the Bible in the chapters which follow, which will help those who are beginning to read God's word and save them from the pitfalls; and will also, I hope, act as a fence and safety net for those who are much further along the way, keeping them in the path on which God's word is a glorious light.

I am grateful to Tony Collins, formerly of Hodder and Stoughton, for encouraging me to write this book. The form it has eventually taken was his suggestion and I have appreciated his interest in its development. I am also grateful to my very good friend the Rev. William Dunlop of St. George's-Tron Church for reading the manuscript and discussing it with me. Needless to say, neither of these friends can be held responsible for the contents! As always I want to express my appreciation to my family for their encouragement and loving friendship which makes writing a book possible!

SINCLAIR B. FERGUSON
Glasgow
October 1981

One

Trusting the Bible

1 Why Have a Bible?

On some ninety occasions in the New Testament the expression 'it is written', or a similar phrase, appears. We are so used to the existence of the book we call 'The Bible', and so accustomed to thinking of it as part and parcel of the Christian life—reading it privately, listening to it read and preached on in public—that we rarely, if ever, pause to ask the question: Why do we have the Bible?

The question itself is far-reaching, perhaps even dumb-founding to Christians who have used the Bible ever since they learned to read. For Christianity is a book religion. Our beliefs, manner of life and day-to-day experience as Christians are profoundly moulded and directed by the contents of some sixteen hundred pages of closely printed information. Yet only rarely do Christians stop to ask: But why do we have a Bible at all?

For many centuries the Bible was not used in the way most Christians today use it, for personal, devotional Bible study. Very few ordinary people could afford to possess a copy of the New Testament until after the Reformation and the development of printing in the sixteenth century. For the longer part of the history of the Christian Church, daily Bible-reading has been the luxury of the few rather than the privilege of the masses.

Why then do we have a Bible, and why is the Christian faith intimately bound up with its contents?

Revelation

The answer is that through the Bible God communicates with men, reveals himself to them, and brings them into fellowship with himself. Simply expressed, it is through the Bible that God makes himself known.

We discover that life takes on a new perspective through the study of great doctrines and spiritual truths unfolded from Scripture. We are helped because we have come to know and understand better what God is like. We now see his hand is on our lives when before we could not understand the trials we faced; we now love him more because we feel that we know him better. This is what the Bible is for. If it does not achieve this goal, then we have not yet begun to use it properly.

Yet there is more to the Bible than this. For the Bible is really more than God's self-revelation to us. It is also God's remedy. It is the divine prescription for spiritual illness. If men had not developed spiritual sickness it is possible there never would have been a Bible. Certainly, if there had been, it would have had a very different story to tell from the one it does.

How then is man spiritually ill? The apostle Paul explains the situation in these words:

Men . . . suppress the truth by their wickedness, since what may be known about God is plain to them, because God has made it plain to them. For since the creation of the world God's invisible qualities—his eternal power and divine nature—have been clearly seen, being understood from what has been made, so that men are without excuse.

For although they knew God, they neither glorified him as God nor gave thanks to him, but their thinking became futile and their foolish hearts were darkened. Although they claimed to be wise, they became fools and exchanged the glory of the immortal God for images made to look like mortal man and birds and animals and reptiles.

(Rom. 1:18–23)

When God made man in his own image (Gen. 1:26–7), he gave him the joy of knowing and serving him. He displayed his own nature in the things that he had made. In this amazing universe he gave man a kind of visible picture of his own invisible qualities and powers.

It is impossible for us to recapture what that must have been like. Perhaps when we watch a magnificent sunset, or sense the grandeur of a mighty animal of the wilds, or look up into the vastness of star-sprinkled space, or wonder beside the cot of a sleeping baby and feel that our breath is taken away with the glory of it all, we touch the outline of what it must have been like to know God through his creation. But then we are always rudely awakened; we remember our fears, our sins, our sorrows and the certain prospect that all these pleasures will be cut short by death. But when man was originally created no such shadows fell on his knowledge of God. The testimony of Psalm 19 recaptures the essence of that spirit:

> The heavens declare the glory of God;
> the skies proclaim the work of his hands.
> Day after day they pour forth speech;
> night after night they display knowledge.
> There is no speech or language
> where their voice is not heard.
> Their voice goes out into all the earth,
> their words to the end of the world.
>
> (Ps. 19:1–4)

All this may still be true (and is, according to the Bible's testimony). But it is certainly not how men see things. Men question the goodness of God, and repudiate his very existence. They say that they see no guarantee of his presence, no foolproof arguments for his existence. As they examine the evidence, they say, all around is in darkness. There is no light in the universe which leads us to God. And so they turn from him.

This comes as no surprise to a student of the Bible. But he realises that the fact of the matter is very different. The darkness is not *outside*, says Paul, but *inside*. No wonder men do not discover God, for they have become futile in their thinking, and their minds have become darkened. The tragedy is that the darkness is inside, not outside! God's wonderful power, and his nature as the living, loving God can still be seen in the things which he has made. Even the marred relics of the original creation still bear the marks of the Creator's loving hand.

This is the poignancy of our lives. Creation cries out in concert to us: God the creator loves and sustains his creation. But men are blind to his revelation, cold to his love, hardened against his will. They do not by nature know God.

Few people have given more thought to this, or expressed themselves more eloquently on it, than the Frenchman John Calvin. Here is what he wrote:

It is therefore in vain that so many burning lamps shine for us in the workmanship of the universe to show forth the glory of its Author. Although they bathe us wholly in their radiance, yet they can of themselves in no way lead us into the right path. Surely they strike some sparks, but before their fuller light shines forth, these are smothered. For this reason, the apostle . . . means . . . that the invisible divinity is made manifest in such spectacles, but that we have not the eyes to see this unless they be illumined by the inner revelation of God through faith.

(*Institutes*, I:v:14)

What God has done is this. He has seen men in their natural inability to know and love him, to understand and serve him, and he has come to their assistance. He has done so by a series of mighty acts, in order to bring men back into the knowledge of himself. Lest even this be misunderstood or distorted, he has given to us his own explanation of these events. He tells us what we may expect in our lives when we trust him, by showing us how he has worked in the lives of people like ourselves over the centuries of Bible history.

The Letter to the Hebrews, which is essentially a book explaining the way in which we can be brought to the knowledge of God through Jesus Christ, opens with a summary of what God has done to remedy the condition of men apart from God: 'In the past God spoke to our forefathers through the prophets at many times and in various ways, but in these last days he has spoken to us by his Son.' (Hebrews 1:1, 2)

The revelation God has made of himself has several important features. First it is historical: God has intervened in the history of the nations in order to show his power and love. Secondly it is verbal: God has given a clear interpretation and explanation of his deeds through those who penned the pages of Scripture. Then, it is cumulative: God gave his revelation in different ways and at different times. And finally, it is Christ-centred: this revelation reached its fulfilment when God spoke his final word to men in the coming of his Son, Jesus Christ.

God has spoken in various ways and at different times. Scripture is the record of this revelation. In some ways it would have been possible to live the Christian life without it. Generation could have passed on to generation the story of Jesus and the apostles. But God has been concerned to preserve the truth about his salvation for us. So he has given us the Bible. He knows that men's memories are short, their tongues are long and their hearts are deceitful. The Bible preserves in a reliable form for us what would have become garbled over the succeeding centuries. The Dutch writer Herman Bavinck put it well by saying:

The written word . . . does not die upon the air but lives on; it is not, like oral traditions, subject to falsification; . . . it is not limited in scope to the few people who hear it, but is the kind of thing, rather, which can spread out to all peoples and to all lands. Writing makes permanent the spoken word, protects it against falsification, and disseminates it far and wide.

(*Our Reasonable Faith* p96)

This reminds us that the Bible is not meant primarily for scholars; it was not given by God to be a text-book in the colleges. It is, rather, God's pastoral book, and has an evangelistic and edifying purpose—not merely to fill our heads with information, but to fill our hearts with the knowledge of God and love for him.

When we understand this we discover that it has an effect on our spirit as we come to read or hear the word of God. We must never allow ourselves to be drawn away from this assurance, that what we are reading is a message which God has specially given and preserved in written form. Through it he tells us how much he loves us, and how he will work in our lives to help us to know and serve him. If we see this, then we will be willing to work hard to understand Scripture, when that is demanded of us; we will be glad to take whatever steps are necessary to become well acquainted with the mind and will of God in the Bible. Then we shall begin to see that passages of Scripture, whose relevance we did not previously understand, have become full of meaning and blessing in our lives.

So far, we have said that the Bible is the record and interpretation of God's revelation in history. We can think about the Bible itself as revelation. But there are two other ideas which we must grasp if we are to understand what the Bible is and why God has given it to us in the precise way that he has. For the Bible itself claims to be both a divine and a human book. It is inspired by God, and yet in its pages he accommodates himself to the understanding of man.

Inspiration

We speak about the Bible as 'inspired'. But what do we mean when we say we believe the Bible is 'inspired by God'? It is probably not unkind to suggest that sometimes Christians have very hazy ideas about inspiration—and rather unbiblical ones!

When we say that Scripture is 'inspired', we do *not* mean that it is 'inspiring'. It is, often. But there are many passages which do not seem to be very inspiring.

Take the opening chapter of the Gospel of Matthew as an example. What would your reaction be if someone tried to preach on that long genealogy of Jesus with which the Gospel opens? How would you look forward to the sermon, if that long list of names was chosen as the Scripture reading? I think it would be fairly accurate to say that the average reaction might be: 'We're in for a pretty dull time of it to-day!' So, from one point of view, the Bible is not always an inspiring book (think of parts of Leviticus, or some of the long harangues in the prophets).

Of course, we can go much too far in saying that. For, whenever we begin to see the real meaning, the reasons why the original writer included what he did in the book he wrote, we *do* find that even obscure passages can be inspiring. When we see the message which runs through the genealogy of Jesus, that 'God is working his purpose out, as year succeeds to year', then we discover how thrilling it all is. Nevertheless, when Paul wrote to Timothy and said that all Scripture is inspired by God, he meant something different from 'inspiring'.

What is inspiration? The great expert on the subject of biblical inspiration in the twentieth century has been Dr. Benjamin B. Warfield, who taught at Princeton Seminary in the U.S.A. It is worth quoting an arresting statement which he wrote:

It is very desirable that we should free ourselves at the outset from influences arising from the current employment of the term 'inspiration'. *This term is not a biblical term*, and its etymological implications are not perfectly accordant with the biblical conception of the modes of the divine operation in giving the Scriptures. (Author's italics.)

(*The Inspiration and Authority of the Bible* p153)

What did Warfield mean? Since he was one of the staunchest defenders of the inerrancy of the Bible, it seems to be an amazing thing that he denied that it was 'inspired'! What he meant was this: we should not think of the Scriptures as an object into which God breathes, but as something which God himself has 'breathed out'. That is why the *New International Version* of 2 Timothy 3:16 adopts the translation which Warfield suggested: 'All Scripture is *God-breathed*'. It is not a matter of God *adding to* what men had written, but of God being the origin, the source of what has been written. Consequently there are several places in the New Testament where, when quoting from the Old Testament, 'God' and 'Scripture' seem to be interchangeable terms. If Scripture has said it, then (since Scripture is God-breathed) we can say: God has said it (see Gal. 3:8; Rom. 9:17 where 'Scripture' is really the equivalent of 'God'; and Matt. 19:4, 5 [quoting Gen. 2:24]; Heb. 3:7 [quoting Ps. 95:7]; Acts 4:24, 25 [quoting Ps. 2:1] where what 'Scripture says' is regarded as equivalent to what 'God says').

Two things are involved in the inspiration of the Bible. First, the Holy Spirit worked through the men who wrote the books of the Bible, and did so in such a way that God's word was communicated in what they wrote. Undoubtedly the writers were in complete control of themselves when this happened. But at the same time they were under the control of the Spirit.

We do not experience the Holy Spirit's power in the same way. But we perhaps do experience his power in a parallel way. We may act in complete control of ourselves, as we walk in the Spirit; but in retrospect discover that his perfect purposes were being accomplished through our action. Indeed, on those occasions when we are most conscious of the presence of the Spirit in our lives, rather than imagine we have lost control, we feel we are more fully ourselves than we have ever been! So Peter says that the writers of the Bible were 'carried along by the Holy Spirit' (2 Peter 1:21) when they wrote.

This is exactly what Jesus promised when he spoke with his disciples in the Upper Room. We tend rather hastily to apply everything he said then to ourselves (a common mistake in our Bible study, as we will discover in a later chapter). But some of the promises he then gave were specially intended for the apostles:

But the Counsellor, the Holy Spirit, whom the Father will send in my name, will teach you all things and will remind you of everything I have said to you.

(John 14:26)

But when he, the Spirit of truth comes, he will guide you into all truth. He will not speak on his own; he will speak only what he hears, and he will tell you what is yet to come.

(John 16:13)

This was the promise Jesus gave to them that there would be such a thing as a New Testament, and they would be responsible for its writing, through the influence of the Holy Spirit.

Secondly, God over-ruled the lives of the men who wrote the Bible. Just as he prepares us for his service, so he prepared men throughout the ages who would be fitted to write the kind of books which now make up our Bible. Again, B. B. Warfield has well described the significance of this:

> If God wished to give his people a series of letters like Paul's, he prepared a Paul to write them, and the Paul he brought to the task was a Paul who spontaneously would write just such letters.
>
> (*The Inspiration and Authority of the Bible* p155)

When, as a young man, Warfield expressed that view, he was accused by some Christians of denying the inspiration of the Bible! The same would probably happen today. Yet that suspicion is a very significant one, because it is rooted in the false idea that because the Bible is inspired it cannot also be truly human, and consequently the writers really played no conscious role in its writing. It is vitally important that we see the mistake involved in this. At bottom it is the product of believing in a God who does not really come down to our level, but who always remains aloof. Such gods are the gods of Greek mythology and first-century heresy, and not the God and Father of our Lord Jesus Christ. Until we recognise the wonder of God speaking to men, and doing so through men, we will never learn to love the Bible and love God for giving it to us. This is precisely the point to which we must now turn.

Accommodation

The fact that the Bible is inspired by God needs to be recognised if we are to adopt a right attitude to it, and hear God's voice in it. But the twin fact, that God has accommodated his infinite wisdom to our level of experience by giving the Bible through men, also needs to be fully recognised if we are rightly to understand its message.

The human characteristics of the Bible are very obvious. It is a composite work, after all, written by various men at different times. Their personalities, backgrounds, concerns and gifts all shine through what they have written. Furthermore, the books of the Bible were composed in very different ways.

How did Moses write the first books of the Bible? Here is a suggestion by the late E. J. Young,

> It is perfectly possible that in the compilation of the Pentateuch Moses may have had excerpts from previously existing written documents . . . (which) might, in *certain cases*, explain the use of the divine names in Genesis.
> (*An Introduction to the Old Testament* p153)

The book of Psalms obviously developed over a long period of time, and reflects, perhaps more than any other Old Testament book, the ordinary human experience and emotions which, under God's loving superintendence, contributed to the spiritual value of Scripture.

The Gospel of Luke is an interesting document, because its author actually tells us how he went about compiling it. Like a student today writing a thesis, he describes his method and aims:

> Many have undertaken to draw up an account of the things that have been fulfilled among us, just as they were handed down to us by those who from the first were eye witnesses and servants of the word. Therefore, since I myself have carefully investigated everything from the beginning, it seemed good also to me to write an orderly account for you, most excellent Theophilus, so that you may know the certainty of the things you have been taught.
> (Luke 1:1–4)

The Bible is a human book from start to finish! Fail to understand this and we miss its message.

A matter of weeks before this book was written I heard a discussion on the radio between two people of considerable intellectual ability which sadly illustrated this point. They were lamenting together the increasing disappearance of the Authorised Version. The reason? Because no other version matched the dignity of its language. New translations by comparison were prosaic. The language was all very ordinary! They saw the purpose of the language of the Bible as the very reverse of God's intention. He wanted to come down to man's level and meet his needs; they wanted the Bible to be removed from common humanity's language and experience. But to do this is to close our eyes to the marvel of Scripture—that God has condescended to speak to his rebellious creatures and show himself to them as a Saviour. So wrote Augustine:

> Scripture proceeds at the pace of a mother stooping to her child, so to speak, so as not to leave us behind in our weakness.

> God speaks through a man, in a human way, because in speaking in this way he is looking for us.

The repercussions of this are two-fold. The first is the influence this has on the way in which we study the Bible. If it is human as well as divine, then we will not study it as though it had fallen down from heaven—the Bible is very different from the kind of book the Book of Mormon is claimed to be! It is necessary for us to enquire into the times, circumstances and experience behind its writing. We need to try to discover what was in the mind of the writer when he wrote, and what he believed he was saying to his contemporaries. All this will help us to discover what God is saying to us today. If we treat this kind of study lightly, it should not surprise us if we end up applying God's word to our lives in a different way from the one he intends.

The second repercussion of recognising the human element in the Bible is this: it will help us to appreciate that it is inevitable that there should be questions and problems about the nature and message of the Bible which we cannot resolve. Since by giving us the Bible God has invaded history, we may find there are as many mysteries about the Bible as there are in trying to understand the person and work of the Lord Jesus Christ. But these are mysteries which should make us wonder and worship—that God has come to us, even when we are men and women of little faith; yes, and little understanding too.

God has spoken. He has come down to our level, like a father communicating with his children. He has humbled himself. That is why when we open the pages of Scripture we too must humble ourselves if we are to meet with this gracious, speaking God. For we cannot really come to know God in his word unless we are willing to be made like him through our study of its pages.

2   Getting It Together

We began the first chapter by asking the very simple, yet fundamental question: Why do we have a Bible at all? We are so used to its existence that we rarely, if ever, stop to ask that question.

But there is another basic question which we should ask. How did the Bible—these sixty-six different books written over a period of many centuries—come to be bound together in one volume?

Were you ever given, as a youngster, a little card with a picture of a book-case divided into a series of sections, each holding several books from the Bible? Were the sections 'history', 'poetry', 'biography' and so on? It was meant to teach us that the Bible is not one single book, but a collection of books, a library of God's truth composed over many years, containing different kinds of literature. But how do we know which books should be in the library? How did the sixty-six we have find their places? How can we be sure we have the right books? Can we add more books to the Bible? And, anyway, what practical difference does it make?

The Thirty-Nine Articles of Anglicanism, and Presbyterianism's *Westminster Confession of Faith* (1643) both tell us that the sixty-six books which we find in our Bibles form the 'canon' of the Old and New Testaments. 'Canon' is a Greek word. It means a staff, or a straight rod. It came to be used, naturally, as the word for a measure, or rule, and so for a rule of action. It is used in the New Testament in this sense (2 Cor. 10:13, 15, 16), most clearly in Paul's concluding words to the Galatians: 'Peace and mercy to all who follow this rule, even to the Israel of God' (Gal. 6:16). During the early centuries of the Church's life, it came to be applied to the contents of the New Testament: together they formed the 'rule of faith and life' by which the whole Church and Christians individually governed their lives.

But how did the Old and New Testaments come into existence?

The Old Testament Canon

Moses was commanded to write down in permanent form the revelation which was given to him by God: 'When Moses went and told the people all the Lord's words and laws, they responded with one voice, "Everything the Lord has said we will do." Moses then wrote down everything the Lord had said.' (Exod. 24:3, 4)

When Deuteronomy records the final period of Moses' life, it tells us about the arrangements he made for the future leadership of God's people. He spoke to Joshua in a great public gathering, ordained him to the leader's office and assured him of the help of God. But he made a further provision for the people:

Moses wrote down this law and gave it to the priests, the sons of Levi, who carried the ark of the covenant of the Lord, and to all the elders of Israel. Then Moses commanded them: 'At the end of every seven years, in the year for cancelling debts, during the Feast of Tabernacles, when all Israel comes to appear before the Lord your God at the place he will choose, you shall read this law before them in their hearing. Assemble the people—men, women and children, and the aliens living in your towns—so they can listen and learn to fear the Lord your God and follow carefully all the words of this law. Their children, who do not know this law, must hear it and learn to fear the Lord your God as long as you live in the land you are crossing the Jordan to possess.'

(Deut. 31:9–13)

Indeed, although God appointed a leader and gave the people a Scripture, he made it clear that the latter always exercised authority over the former. His word to Joshua at the beginning of his ministry is:

> Be strong and very courageous. Be careful to obey all the law my servant Moses gave you; do not turn from it to the right or to the left, that you may be successful wherever you go. Do not let this Book of the Law depart from your mouth; meditate on it day and night, so that you may be careful to do everything written in it. Then you will be prosperous and successful.
>
> (Josh. 1:7, 8)

The word of God, in its written form, as Scripture, became the rule by which Joshua and all the people of God were to govern their lives. It was to be their 'Bible'.

As we read on through the pages of the Old Testament we discover that the whole of Israel's life is determined by their faithfulness, or faithlessness to this command from the Lord. All history is interpreted by that principle; all worship is a reflection of it. The key to understanding the message of the prophets is that they are men sent from God to underline the failure of the people to walk by the word of God; they warn them that the judgments which he promised to the unfaithful are already looming on the horizon of history. The same God who spoke in the giving of the Law is speaking again through the prophets. He calls men back to faithfulness to their covenant obligations and obedience to the Law. Consequently, believing people in the Old Testament period recognised that the same word of God could be heard in the sermons of the prophets as was heard in the writings of the Law.

The Jews appreciated something which often evades Gentile readers of the Bible. They included such books as Joshua, Samuel, Kings and Chronicles *among the prophets*.

They saw that the principles which were so clearly delineated in the preaching of the prophets were just as powerfully present in the way in which the 'history books' of the Old Testament recorded national history. They were written from the point of view of the Law of God. The appearance of prophets like Elijah and Elisha in the chronicles of God's dealings with his people was simply the tip of the iceberg. God was always judging his people in the light of the Law, even when he sent no messengers to remind them that they were rebelling against him.

So already we see that there were two sections to the 'canon', the Scriptures which God was giving to his people. There was the Law, and then developing from it, the Prophets. To these were added what came to be known as 'the Writings'; books like Psalms and Proverbs, the book of Job, Ruth, Song of Solomon, Ecclesiastes, Lamentations and Esther. There is a good deal of mystery surrounding the way in which these particular books came to be regarded as Scripture. The last five books (known as The Five Scrolls) have for many centuries been associated with the great Jewish Festivals. For a long time they were publicly read on such occasions, and used as illustrations of the ways of God with men. They were graphic portrayals of the principles expounded in the Law and reinforced in the Prophets.

We may not be able to answer all the questions about how these different books became part of the Bible. What is clear, however, is that as time passed God's people came to recognise that they transmitted to mankind the authentic voice of God. Despite their differences in authorship, style, type of literature and time of composition, there was a unifying thread running through them. This came to be recognised by the heart of the faithful hearer: God's voice spoke with a consistent authority; the same principles which he had momentously given to the people at Sinai were demonstrated and illustrated in this diverse library of writings.

During the first century A.D. Jewish Rabbis met at Jamnia and discussed the contents of the Old Testament Scriptures. They were not so much seeking to formulate the canon of the Old Testament, as to discuss whether the books generally recognised as Old Testament Scripture were in fact the books which should be so recognised. Much later, during the Protestant Reformation, when the long-accepted teaching of the Roman Church on the canon of Scripture was placed in doubt, there was further discussion of it.

However, for most Christians it is sufficient to know that the Old Testament which we have is, as far as we can say with certainty, the same Old Testament as Jesus himself used. He freely quoted various parts of the Old Testament as the word of God or Scripture. He clearly shared the view of his contemporaries that it was all-inspired and finally authoritative. It was not over the content of Scripture (the canon) that Jesus and the Pharisees were at loggerheads, but its interpretation (and, ultimately, therefore, its authority, since they would not allow Scripture to interpret itself to them). So our Lord spoke of the divine origin of the Pentateuch (e.g. Matt. 19:4, 5); he constantly referred to the necessity for prophecy to be fulfilled; he commented on the way in which David's writing was inspired by the Spirit (Mark 12:36). When he met with the two disciples on the Emmaus Road he began 'with Moses and all the prophets' and explained how their words were but the preparation for his coming (Luke 24:27). Later that evening, the risen Jesus made the position more explicit:

'This is what I told you while I was still with you: Everything must be fulfilled that is written about me in the Law of Moses, the Prophets and the Psalms.' Then he opened their minds so that they could understand the Scriptures.

(Luke 24:44, 45)

Jesus' Bible and our Old Testament were the same. His Bible was not one book, but many scrolls; his Bible was in three major divisions, unlike ours. The books were in different order. But the content was the same, and on that content he stamped his own imprimatur: 'This is the word of the Lord.' What he thought of as God's word we may confidently call 'the word of God' also.

The New Testament Canon

Perhaps you have heard it said (or even thought it yourself), that if the apostles could see how closely their writings are studied, almost two thousand years after their death; or, if they were able to return to the Church to-day, they would be astonished to discover what has happened to their letters. They never expected we would take so much notice!

But, when we open the New Testament itself to see what it teaches us about the attitude of the writers to what they wrote, we discover that the very reverse is true. Nothing would surprise the apostles less than to discover Christians still reading what they wrote. Nothing would sadden them more than to see us so often careless of their teaching. They knew that what they were writing was an addition to the word of God.

That may seem to be an extreme claim, but it is not difficult to substantiate it. It is such an important claim that we must give some further consideration to it.

When the authors of the New Testament wrote, they did so in order to communicate the Gospel to their immediate contemporaries. But in doing so, they were conscious that what they wrote was more than just a personal expression of their witness to Christ. It was to be received and read as authoritative teaching. So, for example, Paul tells the young Christians at Thessalonica: 'I charge you before the Lord to have this letter read to all the brothers.' (1 Thess. 5:27) A similar statement appears at the end of Colossians (Col. 4:16).

At the end of the Letter to the Romans there is another statement which lends weight to this view. Speaking of the Gospel of Christ, Paul says that it is 'now revealed and made known through the prophetic writings by the command of the eternal God, so that all nations might believe and obey him' (Rom. 16:26). These words are reminiscent of what he wrote in Ephesians 3:3–6 about the revelation God had given to him. That revelation is now written down— and is contained in 'prophetic writings'. Paul could never have used such an expression, so similar to the way in which he describes the writings of the Old Testament, unless he had realised the significance of what he himself was writing.

The same sense of divine authority appears towards the close of his lengthy discussion of the place and use of spiritual gifts: 'If anybody thinks he is a prophet or spiritually gifted, let him acknowledge that what I am writing to you is the Lord's command. If he ignores this, he himself will be ignored.' (1 Corinthians 14:37, 38) The test of true spirituality is not the exercise of spiritual gifts, but the cheerful recognition that the word of the apostolic letter is also the word of the Lord! It is difficult to imagine a stronger claim to the New Testament's permanent authority and validity for the Church.

Similar claims appear in the correspondence to Thessalonica:

And we also thank God continually because, when you received the word of God, which you heard from us, you accepted it, not as the word of men, but as it actually is, the word of God, which is at work in you who believe.

(1 Thess. 2:13)

If anyone does not obey our instruction in this letter, take special note of him. Do not associate with him, in order that he may feel ashamed.

(2 Thess. 3:14)

This should not surprise us. The idea of an apostle in the New Testament is that of one who is sent. He is invested with the authority of the one who sent him—in this case Christ himself. That is the reason Paul sometimes defends his apostolic office so strongly (cf. 1 Cor. 9:1 ff; Gal. 1:1; 11–24). It is not because he is concerned about his personal reputation, as he makes clear (e.g. in 2 Cor. 11, 12), but because he is deeply concerned that the Lord's word through him should not be neglected, ignored or despised. He is as clearly an apostle as the other apostles. He conveys the authoritative word of the Master, just as they do (cf. Matt. 10:40; John 13:20; 14:26; 15:26; 16:13–15; Acts 1:2). That is why in Hebrews 2:2 the apostles are compared with the angels who were the go-betweens in the giving of the law at Sinai. Nothing could more eloquently express that what they said was the word of God to the people of God. So, when the Gospel of John was written, its author used the same expression for his own book as he had done for the books of the Old Testament—'it is written' (John 20:31; cf. John 2:17; 6:31, 45; 10:34; 12:14; 15:25).

It is this foundation which makes it possible for the Second Letter of Peter to contain the remarkable statement:

> Bear in mind that our Lord's patience means salvation, just as our dear brother Paul also wrote you with the wisdom that God gave him. He writes the same way in all his letters, speaking in them of these matters. His letters contain some things that are hard to understand, which ignorant and unstable people distort, as they do *the other Scriptures*, to their own destruction.
>
> (2 Pet. 3:15, 16)

Peter places Paul's letters on the same level as 'other Scripture'. The writings which God has given to the Church through the apostles are to be regarded as part of Scripture.

The apostles themselves were conscious that this was

why Christ had called them to their special ministry. It was this which made them unique witnesses to him. Others could speak of his saving power; others could be used as evangelists, pastors and teachers. But they had received a special promise from the Lord Christ, that he would send his Spirit to them to enable them to write the pages of the New Testament. He gave them the authority to pass on a body of literature to the Church in all ages as its rule of faith and life. He had all authority in heaven and earth; they were therefore to go, in his authority, to teach the nations everything he had taught them.

Ultimately, therefore, the contents of the New Testament reflect the authoritative teaching of Jesus himself (see John 14:25, 26; 15:26, 27; 16:12–15; Matt. 28: 18–20).

Naturally it took some time before every Christian in every part of the evangelised world recognised the twenty-seven books in our modern New Testament as God's word. Some Churches possessed only certain parts of the New Testament, and the Letters and Gospels were written at different times and in different places. It was inevitable that small versions of the New Testament should be formed, and different canons appear in various parts of the world. Questions would then naturally arise in one area whether books which were accepted in another area should be incorporated into their own New Testament.

Undoubtedly this process took time. Yet from the earliest period the Christian Church recognised that God had been adding to his word through the apostles. The earliest writings from the second and third centuries show that parts of the New Testament were being used as God's word. By the end of the fourth century it was widely agreed that the twenty-seven books we now call the New Testament were the word of God for the new age of the Gospel.

Relevance

You may well be asking what possible practical value all this has, interesting though it may be. In fact its importance is very far-reaching.

The sixty-six books of the Old and New Testament have been given to the Church by the Lord Jesus Christ and the apostles as the word of God. All of the Bible is the word of God. God speaks through it simply and clearly. It is only through the word of God that God himself now speaks to us. Only what we find in the pages of the Bible enables us to say: 'This is what God says.'

Why should that be of such great significance? Because Christian people, who profess that the Bible alone is their rule of faith and life, that the Bible alone is the word of God, often do not act consistently with their profession. Although they pay lip-service to the view that only the word of God is our guide, in fact they live as though God has other ways of 'speaking'.

I vividly remember leading a summer mission with a number of young people. Late one evening three young men—strangers to all of us on the mission—arrived at our headquarters. 'The Lord has told us to stay with you tonight', they said.

I found it a little curious that the Lord had given our team leaders no intimation of this! Interested to discover what lay behind the 'guidance' these strangers had received, I asked further: 'How do you know the Lord told you to join us?' The answer was immediately given, 'He has told us.' When I enquired further, the answer was enlarged to 'He just told us.' 'Well,' I said, 'I would have thought that if the Lord were planning for you to stay with us tonight he would probably have supplied beds to make it possible—and we don't have a single spare bed for you!'

Hurried discussion brought a change of plan: 'The Lord

is telling one of us to stay, and two of us will go' came the reply.

By this time I thought it might be the part of wisdom to agree to their proposal, but at the same time discuss with them the way in which God leads and instructs his children through life. I tried to suggest to them that God does not normally (and perhaps rarely ever) guide his children by the kind of sudden, inexplicable promptings which these young men 'had experienced. 'How do you know this was God speaking, and not the devil?' I asked, 'how can you be sure?' 'We *are* sure' was the reply.

When people claim direct guidance from God apart from the Scriptures, it is virtually impossible to discuss the matter with them and to persuade them that the will of God is known in other ways. Moreover, even intelligent Christians who are convinced that God guides us largely by inner promptings, hunches and 'feelings', are usually very reluctant to put such guidance to the test, and to bring it to the touchstone of Holy Scripture.

When we come to understand the significance of the canon of Scripture—that God has authoritatively revealed his will for the Church *in the Bible*—one of the blessings it brings to our lives is that we are delivered from a potentially disastrous dependence on hunches and impressions. We are delivered from the 'bolt-from-the-blue' approach to guidance which, for all its apparent spirituality, is as likely to come from our subconscious, or even an evil spirit, as from the Holy Spirit. We will not find authoritative guidance any longer in our subjective feelings, but in the directions, promises, examples and commands of God in the Bible. Every thought we have about what *may be* the will of God we will want to bring to the teaching of the Bible, and examine in its light.

This also has far-reaching implications for the Church today in the realm of spiritual gifts, or 'spirituals' (1 Cor. 12:1). I am thinking particularly of such experiences as visions, or dreams, of the gift of prophecy and speaking in tongues. There is an almost natural tendency in an age like ours (which is characterised by a reaction to sterile rationalism and Victorian morality) to be carried away in a wave of enthusiasm for religious experience. It was in an astonishingly similar situation in the Church at Corinth that the apostle Paul (who knew more about these things than anyone else!) felt it necessary to issue many words of warning. We would do well to listen to what he has to say.

We may be in danger today of attributing an authority to dreams, visions, prophecies and messages in tongues which was never attributed to them by the apostles. Many Christians certainly have looked to these immediate experiences as one of the major ways in which God guides his people individually and collectively.

It may be helpful again to illustrate the point. I have known people who have been told, through a message spoken in tongues, and interpreted, that they were to begin courting, and that their courtship should lead to marriage. Similarly, prophecies may be made about the future sphere of service, or whatever, of a particular Christian. What are we to make of this? In the case of two young people 'directed' to one another by a message in tongues my abiding memory is that it would have been difficult for God to have brought two less suitable people to one another! 'Purely human judgment!' someone might say. But what if the great biblical principles about love, courtship and marriage, and the rich store of instruction about the purpose of God in making us male and female, should suggest to us that two young people would be entirely unsuited life partners for each other? What if, when placed beside the teaching of the Bible, the message in tongues appears a contradiction? Which has the final authority?

In this same general area of experience there is a very salutary story in the Acts of the Apostles. When Paul was at Caesarea, the prophet Agabus (probably the same man who accurately prophesied in Acts 11:28) prophesied that Paul would be taken prisoner in Jerusalem (Acts 21:11). The people pleaded with Paul not to go to Jerusalem. Why then did he go? Because he was compelled by the Spirit (Acts 20:22). Now, it is interesting to notice that when Paul had been at Tyre, he stayed with the disciples for a week: 'Through the Spirit they urged Paul not to go on to Jerusalem' (Acts 21:4).

What does this apparently contradictory account of what the Spirit was saying mean? It means that, even in the days of the apostles, prophetic utterances needed to have objective tests to distinguish what was the will of God and what was merely the utterance of a man and could therefore be prone to error. Where were such tests to be found? In faithfulness to God's revelation through the apostles.

Does this not have something to say to the Church today? We live in an 'instant age'. We are prone to look for a God who guides instantly too, rather than one who has invested his truth in the pages of Scripture, and invited us to discover his will by applying its truth to our own lives. Of course there appears to be something more spiritual about immediate guidance, but remember the words of Paul to the Corinthians: 'I will pray with my spirit, *but I will also pray with my mind*. I will sing with my spirit, *but I will also sing with my mind*' (1 Cor. 14:15). We should say: I will be guided with my spirit—*but I will also be guided with my mind*.

This is what happens if we seek the will of God in the word of God. Instead of narrowing and confining our lives, such guidance makes them strong and stable—and, unlike immediate guidance, it transforms our character. As we will see, it is to influence character that God has given us the Bible. At the end of the day the canon has the most practical of all repercussions.

3 Is This God's Word?

If someone were to ask you: 'How do you *know* that the Bible really is God's word?' what would your answer be?

The message Paul brought to the Thessalonians was received 'not as the word of men, but as it actually is, the word of God, which is at work in you who believe' (1 Thess. 2:13). But how did he know? How can we find this kind of certainty about the Bible?

We come to know that the Old and New Testaments contain God's authentic word to us first of all by the claims which they make, and secondly by the effects which they produce.

The Claims Made by the Bible

Not only is the Bible a collection of volumes, written at different times and gathered together over many centuries, but it is also a single book with a great central theme running through it. That is what is unique about the Bible— from one point of view it is many books, from another it is a single work. Is there a reason for this paradox? There certainly is! The Bible was written by many men at different times. But in the final analysis it has only one source, and one author—God himself.

This is not merely an interpretation which the Church has placed on the Bible. It is also the Bible's own view of itself. Sometimes it is suggested that, because the Church 'compiled' Scripture, it is impossible to speak of 'the Bible's view of itself'. But the Bible does speak about itself: it speaks self-consciously about its own nature. As we have seen already (in 2 Peter) it does so in the awareness that in the days of the apostles the Bible itself was growing and coming to completion.

The Letter to the Hebrews puts it like this: 'In the past

God spoke to our forefathers through the prophets at many times and in various ways, but in these last days he has spoken to us by his Son.' (Heb. 1:1, 2) Here is the New Testament's view of the variety of revelation in the Old Testament, as well as its strong emphasis on the fact that it is God who has spoken through these various channels. Because the author is one, the completed Bible conveys a great sense of unity and harmony.

Paul expresses the position in these words: 'All Scripture is God-breathed' (2 Timothy 3:16). He means that every piece of writing which has the character of 'Scripture' shares also in this feature of the Old Testament Scriptures—the 'holy Scriptures' which Timothy had known since infancy (2 Tim. 3:14, 15)—they have been breathed out by God himself.

Similarly, the Gospel writers believed (as John did) that they were adding to 'what is written'. The New Testament writers were fully aware that they were passing on an authoritative message to the Church. We discover that for them too the Bible was not a series of isolated books, but a compilation of literature through which God was speaking one great message to his people.

When Jesus taught his disciples about the Scriptures, he placed his *imprimatur* upon the Old Testament as God's word. For him, Scripture could not be broken, because it was the mouthpiece of God. That is why, when the disciple takes Jesus' teaching seriously, he is driven to the conclusion that Scripture is God's word. The logical conclusion of any other interpretation is that Jesus' view of the Bible (and therefore Jesus himself) is unreliable and defective.

Furthermore, when Jesus set his special disciples apart for the ministry of being his apostles, adding to the already existing Scriptures was one of the primary tasks he gave them. The Holy Spirit was given to them to help them to write Scripture (cf. John 14:25, 26; 16:12–15). They were sent into the world to teach everything Jesus himself had taught (Matt. 28:18–20). All this we have already noticed.

If there was one specific time in our Lord's ministry when his deepest convictions about the Bible were most likely to come to the surface, it was when he was confronted with the immense pressures of Gethsemane and Calvary. But it is precisely then that we see him recognising the final authority of Scripture in his own life.

Why must he die? 'The Son of Man will go *just as it is written* about him.' (Matt. 26:24)

Why must he be betrayed? 'This is *to fulfil the Scripture*: "He who shares my bread has lifted up his heel against me."' (John 13:18)

Why must he be left alone? '*For it is written*: "I will strike the shepherd and the sheep will be scattered."' (Mark 14:27)

Why must he be so hated? '*To fulfil what is written in their Law*: "They hated me without reason."' (John 15:25)

Why does he not use his power to escape the cross? '*How then would the Scriptures be fulfilled* that say it must happen in this way?' (Matt. 26:54)

These words reflect the profoundest convictions of Jesus. The Christian disciple may be confident that his Lord held the Scriptures to be the inspired and inviolable word of God. What they said was what God said. Whatever his personal inclinations (and his cry in Gethsemane, 'Father, if it is possible, let this cup pass from me' indicates where his natural, human desires lay), he looked to Scripture to discover God's will. That was why he humbly submitted himself to it.

When Christ met the two disciples on the Emmaus road he pointed them to the Scriptures as God's authoritative interpretation of his life, death and resurrection. He did not say: 'Forget about your Bible study now that I am alive!' On the contrary, he emphasised the authority of God's word. He encouraged them to understand and to believe its testimony, even though they had not yet recognised his presence with them. Is it not significant that it was *after* Jesus explained the message of the Bible to them that they began to understand who he was?

We know that the Bible is the word of God. It claims to be so. Jesus believed it to be so. We must now go a step further and ask, What effects does the Bible produce which lead us to believe the testimony it gives to itself?

The Effects of the Bible

The Bible *is* a wonderful book. There may have been a time recently when *The Thoughts of Chairman Mao* outsold copies of the *Authorised Version*. But how short-lived are other best-sellers! The Bible has lasted, and stood the test of time. One reason is that it is great literature. At one time Christians used to place a lot of weight on this:

> Read Demosthenes or Cicero; read Plato, Aristotle and others of that tribe. They will, I admit, allure you, delight you, move you, enrapture you in wonderful measure. But betake yourself from them to this sacred reading. Then, in spite of yourself, so deeply will it affect you, so penetrate your heart, so fix itself in your marrow, that compared with its deep impression, such vigour as the orators and philosophers have will nearly vanish. Consequently it is easy to see that the Sacred Scriptures, which so far surpass all gifts and graces of human endeavour, breathe something divine.
>
> (John Calvin, *Institutes* I.viii.1)

For most of us, who do not find that Aristotle 'enraptures' us, all that may seem a little exaggerated! But Calvin's point is valid nonetheless. There is something unique about the Bible. There are few people who read it with an open mind who do not recognise its grandeur and power. There is, however, more to the Bible's effect on us than this.

When the two disciples whom Jesus met on the road to Emmaus relived their experience after his departure from them, they agreed about one thing: when Jesus explained the message of the Old Testament their hearts began to burn inside. They had felt what John Wesley later did in his encounter with Christ in Aldersgate Street, London. His heart too was 'strangely warmed'. It is ultimately this effect of the Bible that persuades us of its truth and power.

Theologians call this experience 'the testimony of the Holy Spirit'. It is called that because it is so often associated with the witness of the Spirit that we are the children of God (Rom. 8:15).

These two things often (although not invariably) go hand in hand—the discovery that the Bible is the living word of God, and the discovery that through faith in Christ I am now a true child of God, born out of spiritual death into eternal life. Abraham Kuyper, a theologian who became Prime Minister of the Netherlands, was already a young minister before he experienced this himself. He described what happens:

> The veil is gradually pushed aside. The eye turns toward the Divine light that radiates from the Scripture, and now our inner ego sees the imposing superiority. We see it as one born blind, who being healed sees the beauty of colours, or as one deaf, whose hearing being restored, catches the melodies from the world of sounds, and with his whole soul delights in them.
>
> (*Principles of Sacred Theology* p558)

This is what took place in the Acts of the Apostles, when the Gospel spread beyond the bounds of the Jews.

Think of the Chancellor of Queen Candace who had travelled to Jerusalem to seek God, and came away having purchased part of the prophecy of Isaiah. See him in his swaying chariot, gripping the scroll to steady it as he reads in Isaiah 53 of a lamb who is led to the slaughter, and yet is wounded, bruised and chastised for the sins of others. The description grips him; yet it is also puzzling and mysterious. But then a voice beside the chariot enquires: 'Do you understand what you are reading?' It is Philip the evangelist. God has sent him to this seeker after truth. 'How can I understand' replies the Ethiopian, 'unless someone explains it to me?' (see Acts 8:26–40). Philip does, and the man is persuaded that the scroll in his hand is the word of God.

Sometimes God sends a Philip to those who seek to understand his word. At other times he opens their eyes and hearts without any human agent. Many Christians, when asked how they became Christians, where they were when their hearts began to burn within them, or who helped them to begin to follow Christ, will say: 'I was alone, reading the Bible, and it all began to fall into place. I understood, and I trusted.'

I had been reading the Bible for a few years before I was able to say that. I began to read it as a primary schoolboy, thinking that reading the Bible and being a Christian were the same thing. I can still remember being stunned by the words of Jesus: 'You diligently study the Scriptures because you think that by them you possess eternal life. These are the Scriptures that testify about me, yet you refuse to come to me to have life.' (John 5:39, 40) I felt then as though those words had been spoken with my life, and my confusion in mind. I was searching the Scriptures. But I was not coming to search for Christ. From then on I searched for him, until I found him. As I look back now I see that the Christ I found some time later was the Christ who had found me through his word, as I pondered the significance of John 5.

Paul saw this happen on a large scale when he was in Thessalonica. The response to his ministry of God's word was a recognition of the voice of God speaking through his words (1 Thess. 2:13). It was a repetition of the promise of Jesus that when he called his sheep would recognise his voice and follow him (John 10:4, 16).

The same experience has been repeated in countless lives, great and humble. Here is how Augustine, at the age of thirty-two, was delivered from the chains of his own sin and separation from God. It is another example of the testimony of the Holy Spirit. He persuades us of the authority of the Bible as God's word by the way he uses it and the effects he produces by it:

I sent up these sorrowful words; How long, how long, 'tomorrow and tomorrow?' Why not now? why not is there this hour an end to my uncleanness?

So was I speaking, and weeping in the most bitter contrition of my heart, when lo! I heard from a neighbouring house a voice, as of a boy or girl, I know not, chanting, and oft repeating, 'Take up and read; Take up and read.' Instantly my countenance altered, I began to think most intently, whether children were wont in any kind of play to sing such words: nor could I remember ever to have heard the like. So checking the torrent of my tears, I arose; interpreting it to be no other than a command from God, to open the book (the Bible), and read the first chapter I should find . . . Eagerly then I returned to the place where Alypius was sitting; for there had I laid the volume of the apostle, when I arose thence. I seized, opened, and in silence read that section, on which my eyes first fell: 'Not in orgies and drunkenness, not in sexual immorality and debauchery, not in dissension and jealousy. Rather clothe yourselves with the Lord Jesus Christ, and do not think about how to gratify the desires of the sinful nature.' (Rom. 13:13, 14)

No further would I read; nor needed I: for instantly at the end of this sentence, by a light as it were of serenity infused into my heart, all the darkness of doubt vanished away . . .

From there we went to my mother [who had prayed fervently for his conversion for many years], and told her. She rejoiced . . . she leaped for joy, and was triumphant, and blessed You, *who are able to do above what we ask or think*; for she saw that You had given her more for me than she had felt able to ask in her poor and sorrowful groanings. For You had turned me to Yourself . . .

And You turned her mourning into dancing. (Ps. 30:11)

(*Confessions* Book VIII: 29–30)

There is a logic in this, although it is not the logic of this world. In the philosophy of this world it is necessary to prove by rational argument that something is the case before it can really be accepted. That is why, when the logic of this world is turned on the Bible it is able neither to prove nor to disprove that it is the word of God. After all, if the Bible is the word of God—what would be a sufficient proof that this was so? A great theologian of the early Church gave us a better logic when he said that 'only God is a fit witness to himself' (Hilary of Poitiers, *On the Trinity* Book 1:18).

There are many ways in which we can commend Scripture. Our lives should show the marks of the grace of God through our study of it. Yet, although we can explain the Bible's own claims; although we can defend the Bible against attacks (even if C. H. Spurgeon said he would rather defend a lion!)—ultimately we know that there must be an inner work of God in our hearts before we are really persuaded that the Bible is the living voice of the living God, speaking to our deepest needs.

We believe the Bible to be God's word, because it claims to be God's word and because the Holy Spirit, as we read its pages, persuades us by its effect that this claim is the truth. That is why, when we find the Bible under attack, and we try our best to defend it, we have done only part of what is necessary. For ourselves, we must turn afresh to its pages to hear the 'still small voice' of God speaking in it. For others, we must invite them to read its message. Only when they do so, and the Spirit of God testifies to its power, will they see that it is the word of the Living God. When they hear God speaking to them, every mouth must be shut, and all the world made conscious of its guilt before God (Rom. 3:19). That voice which silences theirs will finally persuade them that the Bible's claim is valid. It is the word of God.

Two

Using the Bible

4 Do-It-Yourself

The invitation to the Rally for young people gave the title of the talk as 'The Scarlet Cord'. It was an intriguing title. The cord in question turned out to belong to Rahab, the lady of doubtful reputation who made her home in Jericho at the time of Joshua (Josh. 2). The cord was the one she used as a sign to the invading forces. Their orders were to save those who lived in the house outside of which the cord was hanging. That much I already knew as the speaker introduced the theme of his talk. But his main message was this: the scarlet cord is a picture of the blood of Christ. Only those who are protected by the blood of Christ can be saved.

I have never forgotten the occasion, and often used to reflect on it during my teenage years. The question which troubled me was this: How did the speaker know that the scarlet cord was a picture of the sacrifice of Christ? Was that what God was really saying in Joshua, Chapter Two? I did not know then what I know now.

Since the earliest time after the death of the writers of the New Testament (and perhaps during their lives for all we know) some sincere Christians have understood the main meaning of Rahab's scarlet cord to be the message of the cross of Christ. The First Epistle of Clement, written around the end of the first century A.D., tells us:

> They [the spies] gave her a sign to this effect, that she should hang out of her house a scarlet cord. And thus they indicated that redemption should flow through the blood of the Lord to all those who believe and hope in God. You see, beloved, there was not only faith, but prophecy in this woman.
>
> (*The First Epistle of Clement*, ch. XII.)

But is this the correct way to understand a passage of Scripture?

Here is another example, given by Dr. G. Campbell Morgan:

> He preached on this text: 'So Mephibosheth dwelt in Jerusalem; for he did eat continually at the king's table; and was lame on both his feet.'
>
> It is a beautiful story about David and his love for Jonathan. He (the preacher) made his divisions in this way:
>
> 'My brethren, we see here tonight, *first*, the doctrine of human depravity—Mephibosheth was lame. *Second*, the doctrine of total depravity—he was lame on both his feet. *Thirdly*, the doctrine of justification—he dwelt in Jerusalem. *Fourthly*, the doctrine of adoption—he sat at the king's table. *Fifthly*, the doctrine of the perseverance' of the saints—he did eat at the king's table continually.'
>
> (*Preaching* pp115–16)

What are we to make of these two illustrations?

They do not lack ingenuity! But in neither case does the interpretation convey the true message of the passage. Instead of saying what God says in these sections of his word, such interpretations are emphasising something which has really nothing whatsoever to do with the message of these portions of Scripture. We can go further. We can say that, so long as the kind of principles underlying these interpretations are consistently applied, we will be able to make the Bible say almost anything we want. Only by accident will we ever actually say what the Bible itself is teaching!

These may seem to be very harsh comments to make. But a moment of reflection on the passages in question will indicate that, harsh though it may seem, it is none the less true.

What is the point of the cord in the story of Rahab? It is nothing more than a cord. She was not saved because the cord represented the blood of Christ, but because she came to believe in the God of Abraham, Isaac and Jacob. Had the cord been green, or even black, it would have made no difference to her salvation. Yet, because it is scarlet, by association of ideas it has come to be understood as symbolic of the death of Christ.

Similarly, when we read of Mephibosheth, we are not meant to learn that his life provides us with a potted systematic theology. We are meant to learn about the care and mercy of God flowing through his servant David, and of the importance of remaining faithful to one's vows and promises.

These illustrations could be multiplied almost without end. The mistake they embody is that in them the message of the Bible is made out to be something which lies beyond the words which are used and the realities they symbolise. Events, statements and words come to have second meanings—and it is these second meanings which are accorded primary importance. Sometimes the connection between the grammatical and historical meaning of a verse, and what it is interpreted to mean, can be bizarre in the extreme. It may be subjective and even mystical rather than truly biblical. Yet possibly nothing is more common in private and even public interpretation of the Bible than this. That is why it is very important for us to give some attention to right principles and a right approach to understanding the Bible.

Paul laid down the principles of a right approach to understanding and using the Bible when he wrote to Timothy: 'Do your best to present yourself to God as one approved, a workman who does not need to be ashamed and who correctly handles the word of truth.' (2 Tim. 2:15) The verb for 'do your best' (*spoudazein*) is a very interesting word in this context. Its basic meaning is 'to hurry', and in the New Testament it sometimes conveys the idea of making a strenuous effort. Paul uses it in these senses in

2 Timothy 4:9, 21. In his exhortation to Christian unity in Ephesians 4:3, he urges the Christians to 'make every effort' to maintain it. As though to emphasise the energy involved, he goes on to describe Timothy's approach to understanding Scripture as being that of a 'workman'. The idea of 'dividing' or 'correctly handling' confirms this, because the word is also used of making a road! Paul is conveying a picture of strenuous effort being made in order to interpret the Bible's message properly. It is hard work!

The famous Victorian Bible teacher Alexander MacLaren used to go into his study each morning wearing heavy boots instead of soft slippers on his feet. When asked why he did so, he replied that it was to remind himself that when he was studying the word of God he was engaged in hard labour and toil. There is something in that! Someone has said, with a measure of truth, that 'Half the bad theology in the world is due to suppressed perspiration'—that is, it is the result of not really making the effort, taking the time, exercising the necessary disciplines to try to grapple with what God is really saying in the pages of Scripture. (There are, of course, other reasons for the rest of the 'bad theology'.)

A great deal of the value of our personal Bible study will depend on this. Are we really prepared to work at it? Are we willing to get rid of the crazy notion that understanding the Bible is something which comes without effort—we catch it, rather like the common cold? Are we really willing to be *workmen* in our personal Bible study?

If we are, the next stage is for us to try to appreciate some of the principles which are involved in reading the Bible.

Principles of Interpretation

We shall cover several basic and important principles in the pages which follow, but in general terms the first of

these is one which always ought to be at the forefront of
our minds.

Reading Scripture literally

Scripture is to be interpreted 'literally'. The old
Confessions of the Church tended, rightly, to emphasise
that 'the sense of Scripture is one' (cf. *Westminster
Confession of Faith*, I:ix). By this they meant that when we
have discovered what a text or passage of the Bible actually
says, then we have discovered its *only* meaning. Naturally
there may be different *applications* of its meaning. We may
grasp its meaning more or less fully in relationship to its
context and to other parts of Scripture. But the point is that
Scripture does not have special 'spiritual' meanings which
can only be worked out by leaving aside the plain, grammatical, historical sense of what is being said.

We will appreciate this point more readily if we recognise
that such 'spiritual' meanings and 'spiritual' interpretations
do not have their roots in biblical thinking. They belong
to the world of Greek philosophy and religion. When we
read the New Testament Letters we quickly realise that one
of the false teachings which was invading the Church was
the incipient Gnostic doctrine that there are 'secrets' which
only the initiated can 'know'. There are interpretations
which are 'spiritual'. (In 2 Thessalonians 2:2, it seems that
some people 'spiritualised' Paul's teaching about the general
resurrection, and insisted that it had already taken place.
No doubt there were some Christians who thought they
were 'spiritual' and may have entertained similar ideas.)

There were several reasons for these errors. One was the
Greek philosophical view which assumed that material
things are evil in themselves (hence Col. 2:21). Ordinary,
material interpretations of the teaching of Scripture would
then be very inferior to those which could relate everything
to the immaterial world of the spirit! Furthermore, there

were many fantastic elements in the books of Greek religion. As a result men of any integrity found belief in the historicity of the great 'myths' (as we today regard them) to be impossible. Consequently they 'demythologised' them, and understood them in spiritual rather than literal terms. When Christians from this kind of background turned to study the Bible they brought with them this basic approach and some of these presuppositions. They began to look for hidden rather than plain meanings in the New Testament.

Soon it became common place to look for several meanings in any given passage of Scripture. These were often classified.

There was the *literal* or *historical* meaning—what the passage said when understood by the ordinary rules of grammar. This, as we have hinted already, was regarded as being of secondary importance.

Secondly there was the *moral*, sometimes called the *tropological* meaning—what did the passage have to teach about the practicalities of the Christian life?

Thirdly came the *allegorical* meaning. An allegory is a narrative in which the details of the story have a different significance from their literal one. *The Pilgrim's Progress* is an allegory. The celestial city is clearly heaven; the city of destruction is this world; the burden on Pilgrim's back is the guilt of his sin, and so on. The striking thing about the allegorical interpretation as it was employed (and still is) in the Church, is that it tends to turn narrative details into doctrinal statements. That is why some who have adopted an allegorical interpretation of the parables (which usually have only one or two points of comparison, not many as allegories do) have found great difficulty in the parable of the prodigal son, and have wanted at times to find a sacrificial system in the father killing the fatted calf!

The fourth meaning was known as the *anagogical*, which was closely related to the allegorical, and drew out the significance of the passage for the heavenly pilgrimage.

It has to be said that some of the meanings thus drawn out from any passage of Scripture could be helpful. Some of the doctrines which were expounded were true and biblical. But the disastrous effect of this whole scheme of understanding the Bible was that often it brought out meanings which simply did not exist in the text. It made God's word say things which it did not say (sometimes making the Bible itself look foolish). Furthermore, it stated things which were true biblical doctrines, but which, unfortunately, were not derived from the text under examination. Faith then was in danger of resting on sinking sand! If you believe something on the basis of a text, and that text can be shown to mean something quite different, you are left with no solid foundation for your convictions or creed.

There could be no controlling this system of interpretation. When allegory and spiritualising occur, interpretations multiply! In these things one man's meat will be another man's poison, and so it proved to be.

This point is so very important that it is worth taking time to see it illustrated. Here is how the great early Christian theologian Origen (185–254) understood the parable of the Good Samaritan.

The man travelling from Jerusalem to Jericho is Adam. Jerusalem (naturally) represents heaven. Jericho (naturally) represents the world. The thieves who set upon him are the devil and his emissaries. The priest who passes by is the Law; the Levite stands for the Prophets. They cannot save the man. But then comes the Good Samaritan. This is Christ himself. He places the man on his beast, representing the body of Christ in which he bears our sins. The inn where the man is lodged is the Church; the two pennies represent the Father and the Son. The promise to come back represents the second coming of Christ. Now, who can judge between this interpretation, and other suggestions made in those days and since, that the beast is the Holy Spirit, that the innkeeper is the apostle Paul(!), and that the two pennies represent either the two great commands to love, or, perhaps, the sacraments?

Ingenious, yes. Yet the real message of the parable is not to teach a system of doctrine, but to challenge the life-style of the hearer; to turn his own question ('Who is my neighbour?') back upon himself, by asking 'Who was the neighbour?', and on receiving the right answer, to thrust home the application: 'You go and do the same!'

But let us return to the two earlier illustrations to see how the stories of Rahab and Mephibosheth have suffered a rather similar fate. We saw that the messages drawn out from them were a distortion of their proper meaning. Now we should also be able to see the reason for this. It is the mistaken insistence that the plain meaning of the passage must give way to a 'spiritual' interpretation, which includes in it the entire message of the gospel. It is essentially a refusal to take seriously those words with which Hebrews opens, that God has revealed himself in *various* ways and at *many* times.

When God has himself explained that he did not reveal himself fully in earlier days, it is a great mistake to try to look for such a complete revelation. It simply cannot be over-stressed that the key to understanding Scripture is to understand it 'literally'.

But there is probably no statement which could be more open to abuse and misunderstanding than this! What does it mean to interpret the Bible literally? It means, essentially, to read the Bible with a sensitivity to both its grammatical, or literary style, and also its doctrinal content and purpose.

It is vital for us to distinguish between interpreting the Bible 'literally' (that is, taking the words and statements in their ordinary sense within their broader context) and what we might call 'literalistically' (that is, taking the words in their ordinary sense whether that sense is appropriate or not). Our purpose in personal Bible study, after all, is to understand and put into practice what the Bible actually says, and not what we think it should have said!

There is very little point in our loud affirmations that Scripture is God's word written if we are unprepared to make the effort to hear what it is saying. We mould it and twist it at times to make it say what we want it to, and what will fit into our own preconceived ideas (yes, and theological systems too!). To understand the Bible literally, therefore, is not to insist that there are creatures of unimaginable and impossible features in heaven (as in the Revelation), but to recognise the intention of the writer, the kind of literature he was writing, and the overall purpose of the book he wrote. Thus, in the case of Revelation we recognise that the nearest equivalent we have is probably the brilliant cartoon sketches and caricatures which appear in our daily newspapers. Revelation is not an ordnance survey map of heaven, but a series of larger-than-life illustrations—cartoons if you like—revealing the power and victory of God over all evil forces. Fail to understand this and we fail to understand the whole book.

When we approach the Bible correctly, a whole new world of thrilling, if energetic, study opens up for us. No longer do we approach God's word as a 'promise-box' hoping that some single verse, or phrase, will leap out of the page and hit us between the eyes. We approach it as a book which God has lovingly given us *to study*. There are things in it which are difficult to understand (2 Peter 3:16). There will be much labour in grappling with it. I sometimes picture the student of the Bible as a dog worrying a bone until he has managed to chew every last ounce of goodness out of it! The purpose of our daily reading is not simply to help us to reflect on our own spiritual condition, but to hear what God is saying. God wants us to grapple with the great truths of Scripture because they are life-changing. Our aim is to have an intimate acquaintance with the mind of God as he has revealed it in commands and promises. It is as we see these illustrated through the lives of biblical saints and in Jesus supremely, that we begin to discover what his will is in every situation and circumstance of life. That kind of experience can only be obtained if we are prepared to work at understanding what the message of the Bible really is. How much we need in this matter to hear the ancient rebuke: 'Go to the ant, you sluggard—look at the way he gathers his food' (Prov. 6:6–11)!

Reading Scripture in context

Each word must be seen in its verse, each verse in its context, each context in its chapter, each chapter in its book, each book in the context of its author's other writing, each author in his Testament, each Testament in the context of the other.

When we do this, many things begin to become clear. For example, we do not find it so difficult to understand why there seems to be a tension between Paul's teaching on faith and works, and the teaching of the Letter of James. We realise that these two writers are using similar expressions, but in somewhat different senses, and with very different purposes. Again, we recognise that when Paul uses the word 'law' he means a variety of different things by it. If we apply the principle that the same word in the same kind of context normally means the same thing, we will soon discover the significance of his different uses. We will be saved from the 'concordance mentality' which strings together all the uses of a word, and builds doctrine in that way—not realising that words carry different senses according to the way they are used. So, for example, we find that Paul uses 'law' when he means (a) the Old Testament (Rom. 3:19), (b) a section of the Old Testament (Rom. 3:21), (c) the Mosaic administration (Rom. 5:13, 20), (d) God's normative will (Rom. 3:20; 4:15; 7:2, 5, 7, 8, 9, 12, 16, 22), (e) a principle operating in men's lives (Rom. 3:27; 7:21, 23, 25).

Similarly we find that the word 'flesh' can mean ordinary physical existence (e.g. Eph. 2:15) or it can mean man's nature as tainted and defiled by sin (Eph. 2:3). It need hardly be said that the distinction between the two meanings is very significant, and to confuse them could readily lead us astray in our understanding of the biblical teaching.

When we adopt this approach, one of the things we discover is that the context in which a passage is set often gives us clues both to understanding it *and* to applying it in a practical way. For the Bible is itself a book about men and women who thought about God, lived for him and sought to put his word into practice. It is a fundamentally pastoral book, intended to lead us to the knowledge of God and obedience to his will, 'useful for teaching, rebuking, correcting and training' (2 Tim. 3:16). We find clues about how it should be applied on almost every page.

Reading Scripture according to its literary character

We must always bear in mind the kind of literature we are reading. If we read the book of Revelation as though it were history written in advance, we will misunderstand its message. In all likelihood we will build teaching out of it which is not true to the rest of Scripture. Revelation is a picture book, not a book outlining the future of world history—however disappointing that may seem to us to be!

Interpreting the Psalms

Consider the Psalms. When we read them we discover that they are full of what is called 'parallelism': one phrase is explained in the phrase which follows. An appreciation of this, and the developments which are given sometimes by way of explanation, sometimes by way of contrast, helps us to grasp the sense and the spirit of these poetical writings.

And they are poetical. That means the Psalmist uses different figures of speech. He does not always speak about 'bare facts', as it were. We therefore will always be asking ourselves whether he means something to be understood literally, or perhaps spiritually, that is, poetically.

The appearance of the word 'spiritually' in that last sentence may cause you to sit up! After all, I have been saying that we ought not to 'spiritualise' when we are interpreting Scripture. Now I am saying that the Psalmists sometimes do it!

But the point being made earlier was that spiritualising as a fixed principle is a mistake. But failing to see that a writer is speaking of a spiritual rather than a literal reality is equally a mistake. Here is a constant principle: we are to seek to understand the intention of the writer, in order to understand his meaning. Thus, in the Psalms, if some historical situation is indicated (e.g. the general context of 2 Samuel 11, 12 in the case of Psalm 51), that context will have an influence on the way in which we understand the statements which are made. If some frame of mind is described (as for example in the title of Psalm 102) then we will take that into account when we study the passage. These and other clues will help us, by diligent and prayerful reading, to begin to appreciate the message the Psalmist is conveying.

We will thus come to notice a rather important thing to remember in reading the Psalms. Because they record personal experience, personal and subjective states of mind, while all the Psalms are inspired, not everything which is said in them is necessarily a true statement.

I can imagine that some readers who tend to adopt a spiritualising approach to Scripture, and who also believe in the infallibility of the Bible may be tempted at this point to throw down the book in despair or disagreement! Scripture is infallible. Scripture is inspired. But that does not mean that every statement in Scripture, regardless of context, is ultimate truth. The words of the serpent in the garden of Eden provide an obvious illustration. He assured Eve that, despite what God had said, they would not die (Gen. 3:4). When we understand these words (which are part of the inspired and infallible word of God), in their proper context, we will be driven to the conclusion that they are false. These words were a lie! That should not embarrass us at all. It is not Satan who is inspired, nor his words, but the record God has given us. It will not fail us. But we are failing it, and failing to understand it if we think that because words appear in the Bible, they are true, whatever context they may appear in. This is a very important principle in the Psalms, and one or two examples must suffice to show it.

In Psalm 102, the writer is in a condition of great dejection of spirit. There were several reasons for this. Apparently national affairs were at a low ebb—he speaks of the stones and dust of Jerusalem, and seems to be longing for the day when she would be rebuilt (vv. 14, 16); he personally was in great need, physically and psychologically. But in the middle of the Psalm he says: 'you have taken me up and thrown me aside' (v. 10). That was a natural feeling; we may have known it in some measure ourselves. But was it true? Does God do this kind of thing? The answer must surely be 'no'. The man's mind was unhinged, his perception of God and reality distorted. His great need was to have a proper appreciation of the nature of God—and this is exactly what begins to happen in the Psalm (from v. 12 onward). Yet only when we see that the Psalmist gives a distorted picture of God, can we begin to understand the spiritual therapy which God administered to him.

In Psalm 89 we find a similar instance. This is the Psalm of the covenant with David (vv. 3, 28, 34 etc.). But the complaint of the writer is: 'You have renounced the covenant with your servant and have defiled his crown in the dust' (v. 39). Here is a critical point in the Psalmist's experience. He is accusing God of unfaithfulness! The question is: Had God been unfaithful to his covenant? Is God ever unfaithful to his covenant? Our answer to those questions will determine how we interpret the writer's spiritual condition.

It would require a book to deal with all the principles involved in properly understanding the message of Scripture. It is not the purpose of this one to make that task seem beyond the powers of ordinary readers of the Bible! It is not. In fact most of us pick up these principles as we read, rather than by taking a course in the principles of biblical interpretation! But there are two further areas in which it may be helpful to indicate some of the basic principles of interpreting Scripture.

Interpreting the Prophets

Prophecy is a notorious area for bizarre interpretation. But there are a number of very clear principles which will help us to sail a straight course through many of the difficulties we are likely to encounter.

There are two aspects to the idea of prophecy in the Scriptures. One is, obviously, the common idea of foretelling the future. There are many examples of this in the Old Testament, predicting the history of the people under the Old Covenant, and pointing forward to the coming of Christ and the foundation of the New Covenant. There are also a number of prophecies in the New Testament, from the lips of Jesus and the apostles, and also from others like Agabus of whom we read in the Acts of the Apostles. But, *in proportion*, only a relatively small part of all biblical prophecy foretells long-envisaged future events. In fact, biblical prophecy generally has the character of 'forth-telling' rather than foretelling. And even when it is foretelling, it usually has the contemporary as well as the future situation in view.

Biblical prophecy is usually an exposition of, and a summons to return to, the great principles of faith and life which have their roots in God's covenant. It is invariably either a proclamation of God's faithfulness to his promises, or a summons to fresh consecration to them on the part of his children.

Consequently, when we read prophecy, we must bear in mind three things.

First, it is related to the events of contemporary history. To be understood it must be seen against that background. The first question we must ask is: What did this passage say, and what was it meant to do, to the situation in which it was first spoken or read?

Secondly, prophecy is sometimes conditional (e.g. Jer. 26:17ff; I Kgs 21:17ff; Jonah 3:4ff). On occasion it is a summons back to God's word which, if ignored, will unleash the promised judgment of God, but if obeyed may open the windows of heaven and bring down great blessing upon God's people (cf. Mal. 3:10–12).

Thirdly the prophets inevitably clothed their teaching in the thought forms and ideas of their own time. Otherwise what they said would have been totally unintelligible. Their description of what God would bring about in the future was inevitably expressed in terms of the cultural and religious traditions under which they lived. For that reason it is both legitimate and necessary to understand many of their statements in terms of the ways in which the New Testament itself sees them fulfilled. An obvious example of this is Amos 9:11, 12, which speaks of God's future purpose:

> In that day I will restore
> David's fallen tent.
> I will repair its broken places,
> restore its ruins,
> and build it as it used to be,

> so that they may possess the remnant of Edom
> and all the nations that bear my name,'

declares the Lord, who will do these things.

At first sight these words have a plain meaning. They seem to refer to the national, indeed physical restoration of Jerusalem, and to a programme of national expansion and prosperity. Many Christians believe that God still has some future purpose for the Jewish people, and for the land of Israel. It is natural for them to understand these words to refer to that future period. But if this is how we interpret the words of Amos, we have missed out a vital link in the process of interpretation. We have forgotten the New Testament's understanding of this passage.

When the Council of Jerusalem met, in Acts 15, and had heard Peter's plea for the evangelisation of the Gentiles, this passage was quoted as a decisive factor in the decision which was reached. James stated that the evangelisation of the Gentiles was in agreement with the words of the ancient prophecy. The apostolic understanding of these verses was that they referred not to some future ingathering of the Jews, but to the post-Pentecost ingathering of the Gentiles!

This is not to say that God may not still have a purpose for either the Jewish people or the land. It is only to say that such a conviction will have to find support elsewhere in Scripture if it is to be held. It is not the truth taught by this particular passage. What was evident in the use of Amos by James was that he applied the statement of the prophet to the Church, and the visible prosperity of the spiritual kingdom of God—not to the external, physical nation of Israel. Since in the days of Amos the nation and the Church were, theoretically, two sides of the same coin, the prophet inevitably expressed himself in language which could have been applied either to the physical nation or to the spiritual kingdom. Whenever, therefore, we find the New Testament using an Old Testament prophecy we will only be able sensitively to interpret the Bible if we pay attention to the way in which the Old Testament prophecy is understood.

Interpreting the parables

The interpretation of parables, which form a significant part of Jesus' spoken ministry, is also a happy hunting ground for misunderstandings. The great danger is that we should give so much energy to interpreting the details of a parable that we fail to take seriously the 'punch-line' with which many of them reach a climax.

Parables are not intended to be read as though they were allegories in which each feature of the story has a one-to-one parallel with the world of the spirit. Most of the details are intended to 'set the scene', to convey the general atmosphere in which the message of the parable will strike home with convicting power to the hearer. If we confuse the issues by puzzling over the meaning of the detail, we will find ourselves among those who 'seeing do not see, and hearing do not hear' (Matt. 13:13).

We can take it as a general rule of thumb that each parable contains one main point. In some that may be made in different ways, so that the same general point is applied to different classes of hearers. But normally there will be one featured message in each parable.

With this in mind, there are two things for which we should look as we read them.

First, the scope of the parable. What, in general terms, is it saying? We may be helped in various ways to answer this question. The occasion on which the parable was told is sometimes mentioned. The Good Samaritan provides a perfect example. In Luke 10, Jesus is in a discussion with a legal expert about the way to eternal life. Jesus began to press home God's word to the man's conscience, 'But he wanted to justify himself, so he asked Jesus "And who is my neighbour?"' His parrying the blow to his conscience elicited the story of the man who travelled from Jerusalem to Jericho.

Jesus' story spoke to the man's conscience. It was not merely 'an earthly story with a heavenly meaning'. In fact it had a very earthly meaning indeed. But that meaning was not 'do good to your neighbour'. On the lips of Jesus it was an exposing of the man's heart, a ripping away of his self-justification, an indictment of the externality of the religion of the day. Most of all the parable was a stripping away of the legal expert's defence mechanisms. His question had been 'Who is my neighbour?' Jesus' reply, essentially, was: 'That is not the question. The question is "To whom will you be neighbour?" You cannot say, "There are certain people I am obliged to help because they are my neighbours." You can only say, "By the grace of God I am a neighbour, and will prove to be so wherever there is need."' Instead of limiting our obligations to some people in need, the parable lays upon us an obligation which is limitless in its nature.

On other occasions a parable's purpose is made explicit: 'Jesus told his disciples a parable to show them that they should always pray and not give up' (Luke 18:1). Here we only need to read what is said to know what the general point of the parable is going to be.

There are occasions when the point of the parable will be expressed in the concluding words. Jesus closes the story of the Friend at Midnight with these words, indicating the thrust of the parable: 'So I say to you: ask and it will be given you; seek and you will find; knock and the door will be opened' (Luke 11:9). Similarly the message of the Rich Fool is conveyed in these solemn terms: 'This is how it will be with anyone who stores up things for himself but is not rich toward God' (Luke 12:21). When we notice one or more of these hints, as we read through a parable, we are well on our way to appreciating the point which is being made throughout it. This will help us properly to appreciate the whole of the story.

The second thing which should be noticed in a parable is the point of comparison. Many parables are explicitly described as 'parables of the kingdom'. They begin with the words, 'The kingdom of God is like . . .' As we read them, we should ask the question: What exactly is the point of comparison? It may be the manner in which the kingdom is established. It may be an illustration of the principles which are involved in the life of the kingdom—consecration, prayerfulness, patience, boldness, wisdom, or some other ethical or spiritual quality. It may be the issue of personal decision which is brought before us by the story.

Very often, the essence of the parable is something like this: the kingdom of God operates in *this* way—illustrated in the parable—now, what is your response going to be? Is it going to be like the man in the parable? Is it going to be like the first man in the parable, or the second man? (When some comparison has been made.) This is very clearly illustrated in the parable we usually call The Prodigal Son. In recent times it has become known, probably more accurately, as The Two Sons or The Waiting Father. We miss the point of the story if we do not read to the end and consider the situation of the elder brother. Our Lord told this and two other parables in the context of the complaints of the Pharisees that he welcomed sinners (Luke 15:1ff). The restoration of the younger brother by the father's grace, and the refusal of the elder brother to participate in the celebration are intended to make the hearers (and readers) ask themselves: 'Who am I? Am I like the prodigal, a pardoned sinner? Or am I really like the elder brother, whose heart is cold towards the prodigal, and therefore cold towards the love of God?' The parables not only witness to the working of the kingdom of God, but they demand a response to that dynamic power, and they show us what our present response is.

The doctrinal principle

There is also an important logic to be noticed in Scripture, which again helps us to see the shape of biblical teaching.

God works graciously for men, and on that basis, he summons them to faith and obedience. That format becomes particularly important, and obvious, in the New Testament. Always God's work precedes man's. Always grace precedes gratitude. Always, as a direct consequence, doctrine precedes application in the teaching of the apostles.

That is why, when we turn to a Letter like Romans, or Ephesians, we discover that the 'practical' sections are simply the flowering of the doctrinal sections from which they have emerged. Profound doctrinal teaching demands the ethical and spiritual application. It is also the doctrinal teaching which shapes the ethical teaching. The emphasis is: because God has done this (followed by the explanation of some truth), you should behave like this (followed by the exposition of how the Christian is to behave). Understanding these overall patterns, having an outline in our minds of the general direction in which a writer is heading, and how he is dividing his material—all this helps us to handle God's word with the care and reverence which it merits.

5 For Example

One of the learning techniques which the rapid advance in communications technology has provided is the video-replay. It allows participants in sporting events to 'talk-through' the very incident in which they took part. Thus, for example, a footballer may describe the thoughts which were in his mind when he turned and shot for goal; a golfer may describe the shot which he regarded as the turning point in his round; a boxer may recall the moment he realised that his punches had weakened his opponent.

There is a great deal to be learned from others by this kind of sharing of experience, methods, plans and so on. That is also true in our Bible study. We can help one another very simply by discussing the 'how' of getting to grips with a passage or a book. When we listen to others preaching and teaching, we can learn lessons for our own Bible study by noticing how someone else tackles a passage; how they draw its main teaching together; how they apply it. When we listen to sermons, for example, we are not only learning immediate lessons from the passage or text but we are often unconsciously learning how to (or how not to!) go about the business of our own Bible study. In fact, most of us learn to study the Bible in more or less the same way we listen to others expounding the Bible.

In this chapter, I want to 'talk through' a Bible study with you. I have chosen the Book of Ruth for this purpose, because it provides a good illustration of many of the principles of study within the space of four chapters of narrative.

What is the best way for us to proceed with our study? It is always a good thing to try to take the general lie of the land before we become involved in any detail. When we are studying a relatively short book, like Ruth, we can do this by reading through it quickly, catching the general atmosphere, and appreciating the central direction in which the book unfolds. We can then recognise the significance of some incidents which might otherwise be relatively meaningless to us. Having done this, we are in a position to work more slowly through the chapters.

Chapter One

What is the setting? This will often be our first clue to the rest of the book. Here, as in many other books, the opening words give us the answer: 'In the days when the judges ruled'. What is the significance of this? It tells us that the story is set at some time in the period described in the previous book, Judges. When we turn back to it, we discover that it was a period of great instability. The previous page in our Bible will tell us that 'In those days Israel had no king; everyone did as he saw fit' (Judg. 21:25). Throughout the Book of Judges there are many other evidences of the crises which God's people faced, and of how frequently God had to come to their rescue (e.g. Judg. 2:16–19).

At this point we may wonder whether there is any parallel between those days and the days through which we are living. Obviously some books of Scripture will seem at first glance to have special relevance according to the time and place in which we live. Furthermore, it may immediately strike us that what we have in the Book of Ruth is very different from the Book of Judges. There the story is worked out on a national level; here it is on a personal and individual level. That gives us another clue to the general message of the book. The God who is concerned to establish his people in Judges is also the God who is deeply concerned about individuals. No amount of national need ever distracts God from the situations of his own children, however insignificant they may seem to be, even in their own eyes.

These general thoughts will lead us to examine the rest of the first chapter. What do we find? We discover that although the book is called Ruth, the first chapter is largely about Naomi. In order to understand Ruth's life of faith, the writer seems to be saying, we must first look at the life of Naomi. Only then will we see the full significance of the plan of God. That is a lesson in Bible study and in life already!

What do we discover about Naomi? There are several interesting features, although we may need some help before we have worked them all out! She is introduced to us in the middle of a catalogue of tragedy and sorrow (1:1–5). Notice the names listed in the opening verses. It is often wise to try to find out what Old Testament names mean, as they frequently have significance. Naomi means Pleasant; Elimelech means My God is King; Mahlon and Kilion suggest names like Weakling and Pining. Here is the story of a family who, in a time of economic crisis, left the land of promise (thus betraying the name of the husband); of a mother with the burden of two sons whose health was presumably often an anxiety. Tragedy followed upon tragedy in the death of the father, the marriage of the sons, and their untimely deaths.

Here, obviously, we are faced with a serious question, even if we cannot give an ultimate answer to it. Were these events a divine judgment on this family? As we persist in asking questions like this we will often find that our questions are the very ones which will produce answers from the passage; but there will also be times when we discover that God does not intend to give us answers. There will be times too when we just cannot see the answer, and may have to wait for more knowledge and illumination before a solution becomes clear. But this kind of question-asking approach will often lead us to the heart of the matter.

As the story continues we discover a fresh development in Naomi's life. She prepares to return to the land of promise (v.6). There is surely significance in this. Returning to the land of promise is a theme which often appears in the Old Testament, because the land is bound up with the promise of God in his covenant. It is there, and there alone, that he has promised to bless his people. Furthermore, as the passage tells us, it is there that God was blessing his people (v.6). What we have here, then, is a picture of one of God's children who has been separated from all the ordinary means of grace, returning to him. Whether the tragedies of Naomi's life are to be read as a judgment or not, we can now see that God had used them to bring her back to fellowship with himself and his people.

This is a major lesson in the character and strategy of God. It is the kind of area of Bible study where we may want to pause and to pursue the theme much more thoroughly. We will certainly want to pause to reflect on the Lord's dealings with our own lives, and to ask the appropriate questions: Is God dealing with me like this? Have I known his hand on my life in this way? Does this shed light on my experience, or does it help me to accept some situation in which I have found myself? It certainly teaches me that God is prepared to permit many mysterious things in order to draw his children back into his arms. We may notice that at the end of the chapter Naomi is very conscious of the humbling hand of God upon her (v.21—'The Lord has afflicted me'), but she also recognises divine purpose and grace in it (v.21—'I went away full, but the Lord has brought me back empty').

The central section of the chapter (1:16–18) presents us with a rather different scene. Here Naomi stands at the crossroads between Moab and Bethlehem, her two daughters-in-law with her. The first thing we notice is that her own spiritual restoration and her new desire to be with God's people have encouraged her to become a witness to others. She is no longer silent about the implications of belonging to the people of God! The cost of such discipleship proves to be too much for Orpah. We can hardly avoid noticing what was the precise issue at stake; Naomi underlines it in verses 11–14. It is the question of marriage. That raises a major issue for many Christians. Are we willing to go with Christ's people at such a cost? Here again we will want to pause for more reflection, self-examination and prayer.

Would our response have been that of Ruth? Hers is given in the most famous words in the whole book. But often we will find in our study that famous words need to be considered carefully. As we reflect on Scripture, and on the kind of language involved in Ruth's words, we will begin to realise that more is involved in them than an exquisite expression of personal friendship and loyalty. Her statement is often taken at that level. But it should ring other bells in the minds of Bible students. For her words are strongly reminiscent of God's covenant promises (e.g. Exod. 6:7) in which he promises to be the God of his people and binds them to himself. What Ruth is doing here is yielding herself in a personal covenant with God. She is, in essence, responding to the promise of the Old Testament gospel, and entrusting her entire life into God's hands. She is, in short, being converted.

Again we will want to pause for practical reflection. Notice that only now has Naomi's testimony been used to bring Ruth into the covenant people of God—despite the closeness of their relationship over a long period of time. Only now has the blockage been removed, and God's grace has begun freely to flow to others. There are some searching personal questions to ask about ourselves here, surely. Then we will want to consider this issue: Is this what my faith in Christ means? Have I begun to appreciate that God is my God and I belong to his people? What can this mean for me?

So Ruth returns with Naomi to Bethlehem (vv.19–22). The whole town is stirred. Should that not always be the response when God's children prove to be as faithful to him as Ruth and Naomi? How far we have to go to evoke this response! So, as we close our first study, we find ourselves humbled under the word of God, praying that he will use his people to make similar impressions on the world around them. We will pray that a similar witness may be seen in our lives.

Chapter Two

The second chapter begins with a statement which sets the tone for the verses which follow. Boaz is introduced. Just as Ruth's story has to be traced back to the ways in which the hand of the Lord came first upon her mother-in-law, the editor of the Book of Ruth is now telling us that God had another dimension to his plan. Editorial comments like this in Scripture are intended to be signposts. They help us more fully to appreciate the significance of what follows. Here the lesson is clear. God's purposes in our lives involve the gathering together of many strands of his work in the lives of others. Here is a lesson to lead us to wonder and worship. Can we apply it to our own lives, as we trace God's patterns through them?

If the editor alerts us to the fact that we must keep our eyes open for the providences of God in our lives, we do not need to read far before we discover that sometimes these can be hard to bear. Ruth and Naomi were virtually destitute. Consecration to God, we learn, is no guarantee that life will be free from hardship and difficulty (did they reflect for a moment that life might well have been more comfortable back in Moab?). Why is this principle so vital to learn? It may save us from a view of spiritual life which will lead to untold disappointment. Often biblical teaching is given to us not only to deal with our present situations, but to provide the kind of knowledge of God's ways which will give backbone to our lives in days of darkness or difficulty. Forewarned is forearmed!

Can we now imagine ourselves in the position of these women? What would our own reaction be? What has been our reaction to similar difficulties? These are the questions which may help us to see in a new light the gracious working of God in our lives. Are we sometimes made bitter? or perhaps paralysed into inactivity? We can think of others in Scripture who were—like Jeremiah (Jer. 20:7) or the Psalmist (Ps. 102:10). But these women seem to manifest a spirit of contentment despite their condition. Their example sets me thinking in my Bible study about how this can be developed in my own life. It will send me to passages like Psalm 131 and Philippians 4:11, 12.

Ruth went gleaning (v.2). What is the real significance of this gleaning? We may need the help of a concordance, or dictionary of the Bible, to discover that God had made provisions for gleaning in his law (Exod. 19 and 23; Deut. 24:19). Here is another very practical lesson for me to learn. When Ruth and Naomi were in difficulties they found the answer to their needs by living within the boundaries and provisions of God's law. As we read on in the story we discover that this was the pathway which led them not only to God's provision for their present needs, but to the fulfilment of his ultimate purpose for their lives. That purpose, as the closing verses of the book reveal, had repercussions for the rest of God's saving plan throughout the whole of history!

The story begins to unfold. Boaz helps the women, and provides for their needs (vv.5, 16, 17). His life is worth a study of its own. Who was he? What qualities does he display that we should ask God to help us to imitate? We know from our initial reading of the book that he is going to marry Ruth. But what characteristics of his life made him a suitable partner for this young widow who had so clearly consecrated herself to the service of the kingdom of God and his people? If we check up on his family tree we find that he was not a 'pure' Jew at all. He was in fact a descendant of Rahab the harlot, as the New Testament shows (Matt. 1:5). Did his own family background and personal experience fit him to take a special interest in, and develop a special affection for this Moabitess? No detail even of our family life is accidental or incidental where God is concerned!

From time to time in studies like this it can be a helpful thing to step back from the immediate action to try to sense the plan which God has been pursuing in this historical narrative. Had these two women not lost their husbands, they would probably never have returned to Bethlehem. Had they returned full, Ruth might never have evidenced the gracious qualities which she did. Had she never gleaned, the story would not have begun to take the surprising turn which it did. None of this could be anticipated when we read the first lines of the book. God's providences, said a wise man, are like Hebrew words—they can only be read backwards! We will remember Jesus' words to his disciples: 'Afterwards you will understand' (John 13:7). If we have learned that lesson from our study of Ruth 2 we will have learned a great deal. We will be able to say with Naomi: 'The Lord has not stopped showing his kindness' (2:20).

Chapter Three

The Bible comes to us from a very different world from our own. We live in a totally different environment, geographically, intellectually, historically and culturally. Relatively few features of life have remained static since the Book of Ruth was written. We know that the human heart is the same; we know that God and his ways with men are the same. The question, indeed the problem, which sometimes confronts us in our study therefore is: How do I translate what God did in that world into what God is doing in our world?

From time to time interpreting God's word for our own lives and times will demand that we familiarise ourselves with the cultural world of the Bible. We had to do this in Chapter Two of Ruth, in order to understand the significance of gleaning. In Chapter Three another Old Testament principle lies behind the story. Mention is made here of the 'kinsman redeemer' (cf. v. 12; also 2:20; 3:2).

Again, at this point, we will probably need either a Bible dictionary, commentary, or some very good cross-references in the margin of our Bible. Using these aids we will discover that a much greater emphasis was placed on family life in the Israelite world than in our own. The blessings and stability this brought were balanced by corresponding responsibilities to help a member of the family who was in need. For example, someone might be forced to sell land to pay debts. In this case, a member of the family (the kinsman redeemer) was expected to raise the purchase price, so that the property could be kept within the family, and possibly bought back at a later date if circumstances allowed. We see a reflection of this in the way Boaz treats Ruth in Chapter Two (cf. 2:20).

But there was another institution built in to Jewish family life by the Law of God. It is known as levirate marriage. If a man died childless, his brother would marry the widow and their first son would be counted as the son of the dead man. Because of the complex circumstances which could be involved, this responsibility seems to have spread beyond the immediate relatives and devolved on the kinsman redeemer. It is the knowledge that Boaz was a kinsman redeemer which seemed to raise Naomi's hopes in 2:20 that God might have some special purpose in this apparently accidental encounter between him and Ruth.

Chapter Three recounts how Naomi told Ruth to respond

to the new situation. Ruth is to wash and perfume herself, put on her best clothes, and, after the evening festivities, go to the place where Boaz is lying. There she is to uncover his feet and lie down quietly. When Boaz awakes, Ruth invites him to spread the corner of his garment over her (v.9). This seems to have been the equivalent of a proposal! (See Ezek.16:8.) Boaz points out that there is in fact a kinsman nearer to her than himself, but promises that, should he refuse to marry Ruth, then he (Boaz) will do so.

At first sight this chapter appears to be a less fertile area for Bible study than Chapters One and Two. But there are several very practical avenues of thought for us to investi-gate. Here, after all, is the outstanding story of courtship and marriage in the Old Testament. What can it teach us about this most prized of all human relationships? Are there principles here which will provide instruction for us?

It is interesting to remember how Naomi spoke about the significance of marriage in 3:1. The word she used was 'home' or 'rest'. That points us back to the similar ex-pression in 1:9. The idea carries with it, obviously, the stability, purpose, assurance and strength which a home gives.

This is not to say that the Bible's view of a wife's life is that she should always be at home in the kitchen. See Proverbs 31:16 for the 'ideal wife' who also deals in real estate as a part-time venture, and then moves into viti-culture! Not only this, but she is a successful business woman (v.18). But it teaches us something about one of the great basic needs of a young woman, and which husbands, or prospective ones, should regard as one of their great responsibilities in entering into a marriage covenant. This is brought out rather beautifully in the picturesque invitation of Ruth to Boaz to 'spread his wings' (literally) over her. This may lead us to turn to Ephesians 5:25ff, to meditate on the New Testament exhortations to husbands to love and care for their wives.

A further issue which emerges in these verses is the mutual love and respect which clearly had begun to exist between Ruth and Boaz. Here again we will be reminded of Ephesians 5:33. We will notice Boaz' chasteness (v.13b, 14); his integrity to his fellows (v.12); his kindness to Naomi—his prospective mother-in-law! (v.17); his sense of God (v.13, perhaps also in his prayer in v.14). Boaz sums it up in verse 10. This love is more than a passing attraction.

There is undoubtedly a great deal of instruction here for different ages and stages in the Church. There is a pressing need for us today to be learning these biblical standards all over again. So we find that, for all the apparent culture gap between ourselves and the days of the Judges, God's word still speaks to one of the most basic issues in our contemporary society.

A second line of thought we may want to pursue in this context is the way in which this chapter tells us something about the importance of true character and integrity in all our dealings. We add nothing to God's purposes by snatching at what we may most deeply desire. Undoubtedly Boaz found his emotions stirred by Ruth. He says as much in verse 10. But he also recognises the duty of faithfulness to God, his law, and other men. Boaz, by contrast with so many of us, recognised that the way of blessing must always be the way of principled obedience to God's word and law—whatever we gain or lose in the process. If we know the book of Ecclesiastes we will be reminded of these words: 'Better one handful with tranquillity than two handfuls with toil and chasing after the wind.' (Eccles. 4:6)

Interestingly, Ruth is described as 'of noble character' (3:11). Here we may want to take the time to re-study the pattern of her life and to discover what qualities go to make up such spiritual nobility. Do we not see the need for a truly Christian nobility to shine through our lives in contemporary society? The same truth is reflected in Naomi's comment about Boaz: 'the man will not rest until the matter is settled today' (3:18). Here we have commitment and concern rolled into one. It may be that this is one evidence of the grace of God in the heart which we ourselves are lacking. Our study of Ruth Chapter Three will therefore make us pray that God will work noble character and true grace into our lives and into all our relationships, particularly those which we count most important.

Chapter Four

We come to the final section of our study in Ruth. So far we have been able to trace the character of God and his providential leading of his children through dark experiences. We have recognised also the lineaments of the character of a true disciple in each of the three main characters in the book. Now we discover in Chapter Four that the sad beginning of the story eventually leads to a happy and unexpected ending. Again much of the interest is centred on Boaz. Perhaps we have assumed that Ruth is a story with practical relevance for women only! We will know better by this stage in our studies. In Chapter Four, several further features of his life impress important spiritual lessons on us.

Boaz exhibits a strong trust in the goodness of God. We saw hints of this in Chapter Three, but now they come very clearly to the surface. There is no doubt that he wants to marry Ruth (3:13). But the opening verses emphasise that he believes that if he walks in his duties to God, prescribed in the Law, only what is for his ultimate good and blessing will result. He had no guarantee that this would be the same as his own natural aspirations. But perhaps he had enough experience of God's dealings with him to say to himself:

> Hast thou not seen
> How thy heart's wishes have been
> Granted in what he ordaineth?

As we reflect further on Boaz, we will come to recognise that he displays the combination of activity and patience which only obedience to God's law is able to produce in us. He acts; but since he acts in accordance with the guidelines which God had set out in his word, and does not overstep them, he is restrained from taking matters into his own hands. There are many practical applications of this principle. In our private study, we will inevitably find ourselves examining many situations in our own lives where we have failed. Perhaps we are already in a situation in which this great principle sheds light on the path which we must follow in the immediate future.

When we reflect on the experience of Ruth and Naomi recorded in this chapter we find that it illustrates the great promise of Jesus. No disciple who makes sacrifices in order to serve God is ever ultimately the poorer (Luke 18:29). Ruth had left home and family for the sake of God and his covenant grace; she received *in this world*, home and family, joys and fulfilment which she would otherwise never have known. Here is a line of thinking which will certainly lead us to self-examination, but at the same time should encourage us in thanksgiving and praise.

The response of the elders to all this—recorded in 4:11, 12—is extremely interesting. Here is a picture of the community of God's people seeking to know his will together. It hints at many lessons for our lives as members of Christian fellowships, in the mutual care, respect, affection and prayer which it represents. What is particularly striking is the way in which the concern and prayer of these men are steeped in the thought-forms of Scripture itself. In effect they are doing exactly what we also do in our Bible study: they are reflecting on the grace and goodness God had shown to his children in the past. They trust him as the unchanging faithful Father of his people, to demonstrate the same power and love in the lives of Boaz and Ruth. What a lesson for our corporate praying!

The conclusion of the book yields the most remarkable lesson of all. Boaz becomes a father, Ruth a happy mother, Naomi a delighted granny! It is a 'happy-ever-after' ending. Indeed, that is more profoundly true than we might think. For the book ends with a genealogy. But what a genealogy! It tells us that 'Salmon [was] the father of Boaz, Boaz the father of Obed, Obed the father of Jesse, Jesse the father of David.' The family trees in Matthew 1 and Luke 3 underline the fact that this short genealogy eventually leads to the birth of Jesus, the Saviour. The greatest privilege for the three characters in the Book of Ruth is that they became essential links in the chain which would ultimately lead to the fulfilment of God's covenant promise to Abraham, and to the coming of the kingdom of God. The outworking of God's eternal plan was dependent on the fulfilment of its details in the lives of these apparently insignificant people. Further, their present obedience to his will was the gate through which greater blessing would come. God works in our lives not only for our own time, but for generations yet unborn. This is the great lesson. The challenge is obvious. Do we have a sense of the immense privilege God has given us by taking us up into his purposes? Are we willing to yield ourselves entirely to his will?

So, our study in Ruth comes, for the moment at least, to an end. We will want to move on to another book and grapple with the rich nuggets which God will help us to quarry from it. We have not yet learned everything there is to learn from this one short book. But we have learned something. It will help us to feel that God has yet more light to break out of his word.

Three

Living By the Bible

6 What's the Use?

In Chapter Three we noted that one of the things which convinces us that the Bible is God's word is the effect which it produces. As we read its pages we become conscious that the living God speaks to us through it. We find Christ in it. Indeed, that is why we read it. We go to the Bible as the shepherds went to the manger, as Martin Luther liked to say—to find Christ. Whenever we read it, we want to have some sense of the burning heart which the disciples experienced on the Emmaus road when they began to see how the word of God bears consistent witness to Jesus as our Saviour and Lord.

But if the Bible shows us Christ, it is bound to have very radical and lasting effects on our daily lives. In particular its teaching and general influence will inevitably shape and mould our character. As we delve more deeply into its teaching, we will begin to realise that this is one of the major purposes for which God has given us his word. That fact is brought out clearly in one of the New Testament's greatest statements about the nature and function of the Bible in the life of the Christian:

As for you, continue in what you have learned and have become convinced of, because you know those from whom you learned it, and how from infancy you have known the holy Scriptures, which are able to make you wise for salvation through faith in Christ Jesus. All Scripture is God-breathed and is useful for teaching, rebuking, correcting and training in righteousness, so that the man of God may be thoroughly equipped for every good work.

(2 Tim. 3:14–17)

This is a very remarkable and important part of Scripture, for many reasons. It contains the last recorded words of the apostle Paul, and therefore is likely to be an expression of some of his deepest concerns. It is written to Timothy, the young man (probably in his late twenties or early thirties) who had come to mean more to Paul than anyone else (cf. Phil. 2:19–22). He, above all others outside the apostolic band, was to continue the labours of the mighty apostle. Set, as he was, in the teeming city of Ephesus (1 Tim. 1:3), he faced many difficulties and problems, outwardly in the paganism around him, inwardly in problems in the church, and apparently also in his own life. He needed Paul's wisest pastoral counsel.

What Paul said to him was this: 'Believe God's word, because it has come from him and carries his authority. You know that it has brought you to Christ and taught you the way of salvation. You have seen the effect it has had on the lives of others—your grandmother Lois and your mother Eunice (2 Tim. 1:5), who taught you its truth when you were a child. You have seen how it has moulded my life and sustained me against the greatest odds. You can trust it to do the same for you as well!'

John Calvin once wrote that 'The Scriptures obtain full authority among believers only when men regard them as having sprung from heaven, as if there the living words of God were heard' (*Institutes*, I.vii.1). Timothy was convinced that this was so. He had the evidence of others' lives to prove it. But Paul wanted to urge on him the effect which his study of and obedience to God's word would have on his life as well. So, he added to his statement of the God-breathed character of Scripture an explanation first of the purpose and secondly of the effect of the Bible in the Christian's life.

The Purpose of the Bible

The most vivid description Paul ever gave of the Bible was that it is 'the Spirit's sword' (Eph. 6:17). He pictures the Bible as an instrument, or weapon in the hand of the Spirit, as well as in the hand of the Christian. The Spirit uses the Bible to gain ground in the personality and character of the believer; to cut down offending characteristics in our lives; to slay opposition to the kingdom of God. In another passage, we are told that:

The word of God is living and active. Sharper than any double-edged sword, it penetrates even to dividing soul and spirit, joints and marrow; it judges the thoughts and attitudes of the heart. Nothing in all creation is hidden from God's sight. Everything is uncovered and laid bare before the eyes of him to whom we must give account.

(Heb. 4:12, 13),

God is described in the New Testament as the great cardiologist—the supreme heart specialist, as it were. Indeed, the word which the New Testament uses goes further; it describes him not merely as the one who makes the heart his study, but the one who knows the hearts of men. He is not only a spiritual cardiologist, but a spiritual cardiognostician! (See Acts 1:24; 15:8.) He uses his word to lay bare the deepest recesses of our lives and personalities ('dividing soul and spirit, joints and marrow'), and begins to rebuild our lives like Christ's—*from within*. It is as we come to know God in his word and truth that this amazing transformation begins to take place. Paul again describes this work in two vivid passages:

But whenever anyone turns to the Lord, the veil is taken away. Now the Lord is the Spirit, and where the Spirit of the Lord is, there is freedom. And we, who with unveiled faces all reflect [or, contemplate] the Lord's glory, are being transformed into his likeness with ever-increasing glory, which comes from the Lord, who is the Spirit.

(2 Cor. 3:16–18)

Paul is here contrasting the spiritual blindness of his contemporaries with the transformation which begins to take place in the lives of those who have been made 'wise for salvation through faith in Christ Jesus' (2 Tim. 3:15). They see Christ in Scripture, and by the work of the Holy Spirit their lives begin to take on the likeness of Christ—gloriously.

You were taught, with regard to your former way of life, to put off your old self, which is being corrupted by its deceitful desires; to be made new in the attitude of your minds; and to put on the new self, created to be like God in true righteousness and holiness.

(Eph. 4:22–24)

How had they been 'taught' this? How had they been 'made new' in the attitude of their minds? By apostolic doctrine and teaching! By that instruction which has now been handed down to us in the New Testament. When taken up by the Holy Spirit, this is what leads to the transformation of Christian character!

If we now return to Paul's words of encouragement to Timothy, we will see clearly the ways in which God achieves this great purpose in our lives. He says that the word of God is useful for four things.

Teaching

It is a mistake to think that Christianity is 'caught, rather than taught'. True, we do not become Christians merely by being taught about the Gospel. But we do become

Christians when we are inwardly taught by the Holy Spirit, and when we 'learn Christ' as our forefathers would have said. We become followers of Christ through this inward teaching, or 'anointing' (1 John 2:20). It is invariably associated with our learning the message of the Bible. When we become Christians, we also become disciples, or learners. We place our lives in the hands of Christ and he teaches us through his word. We do not automatically or intuitively come to know everything about being a Christian. There are many things about the Gospel we cannot learn by experience alone. We need the word of God to teach us.

This is one reason why, when we read about the Lord Jesus in the Gospels, he is often to be found *teaching*. When men addressed him, they referred to him as 'Teacher', not simply out of respect for him, but because he regularly taught them about God and man, and did so (unlike their ordinary instructors) 'as one who had authority' (Matt. 7:29). The Saviour Jesus is also the Teacher Jesus. He came to be the Priest and King of his people, to sacrifice himself for them and to rule over them; but he also came to be their Prophet, and to speak and teach the word and truth of God. That is why so much of the Gospel record of his life deals with what he said. He preached sermons, he told parables and applied them. We read of him that 'opening his mouth *he taught . . .*' (Matt. 5:2, literal translation).

When we read about the success of the early Church and its evangelism, we find the same emphasis. The apostles went everywhere teaching and preaching. Paul described his ministry in Ephesus to the elders of the church there, in terms of his public and private *teaching* (Acts 20:20). Again and again in the Letters there is this same emphasis (Col. 1:28). The people of God need to be taught, and the source of the teaching they are to receive is the Holy Scripture.

But, we may ask, why is this teaching so necessary? Why

this consistent appeal to the mind of the Christian? There are at least three important answers to these questions.

First, the New Testament tells us that, by nature, our minds are darkened and need the light of the gospel to illumine them (John 12:35; Rom. 1:21; Eph. 4:18; Eph. 5:8). When we become Christians, we enter into the light and begin to walk in it (Eph. 5:8ff; 1 John 1:7). But obviously the light of the gospel takes time to penetrate our lives and to dispel all the darkness. As Christians we continue to have thoughts of which we are ashamed. We also have attitudes which are ill-informed, distorted and sometimes sinful. At times, unfortunately, we find ourselves in the position of the Hebrews who needed to be taught the first principles of God's word all over again (Heb. 5:12).

Secondly, there are times when our minds are *deceived*. We can have wrong thoughts about Christ, for example. We may believe some action to be sinful which, in fact, the Bible regards as legitimate. We may bind our conscience to some course of action and only at a later stage discover that to do so was inconsistent with our profession of Christ. That is why the New Testament regularly warns us about the danger of being deceived. We can be deceived by riches (Mark 4:19), by men (2 Thess. 2:3), by ourselves (1 Cor. 3:18; Jas. 1:22), by sin (Rom. 7:11; Heb. 3:13), and by Satan (Rev. 12:9; 20:3, 8, 10). The warning note is struck: do not be deceived (Matt. 24:4; 1 Cor. 6:9; 15:33; Eph. 5:6; Gal. 6:7).

That warning is important. Sin would not gain such ready access to our lives if it were not able to appear in an attractive guise! After all, it was the pleasures of sin which Moses turned his back on (Heb. 11:25), and he was able to do so because he was not deceived about how long they would last. He had been taught by God that they were fleeting.

John Owen, whose massive writings display a knowledge of the psychology of sin which has probably never been equalled, described sin's deceiving ability in these quaint, but realistic terms:

> Now sin, when it presseth upon the soul . . . will use a thousand wiles to hide from it the terror of the Lord, the end of transgressions, and especially of that peculiar folly which it solicits the mind unto. *Hopes of pardon* shall be used to hide it; and *future repentance* shall hide it; and *present importunity* of lust shall hide it; *occasions and opportunities* shall hide it; *surprisals* shall hide it; *extenuation* of sin shall hide it; *balancing of duties* against it shall hide it; *desperate resolutions* to venture the uttermost for the enjoyment of lust in its pleasures and profits shall hide it. A thousand wiles it hath, which cannot be recounted.
>
> (*Works* VI:249)

When we are under such pressures (and we are all under some of them), mere knowledge of the Bible alone will not protect us. But without that knowledge there will be no protection at all. If we fail to use the Spirit's sword which enables us to unmask the deceitfulness of sin, then the battle to serve Christ will be lost without a blow being struck in our defence. But if we have learned from the teaching of Scripture to be on our guard, to distinguish between what is true and false, right and wrong, good and evil, God and Satan, then it will be possible for us to stand 'in the evil day', and at the end of it to remain standing (Eph. 6:13).

Thirdly, the mind is the key to the Christian life. If our minds are dull and lifeless, then our Christian lives will reflect that. If our minds are full of thoughts about Christ, then, correspondingly, our lives will show that he is the centre of our attention and that we live for him. But there is only one source available to us from which we can draw information about Jesus. There is only one book which authoritatively instructs us about him; one book through which he has promised to speak with a living voice. If the mind is the 'key' which unlocks the Christian life, it has to be inserted into the 'lock' of Scripture. It has to be 'cut' according to its pattern. We are urged to share the mind, or attitude of Christ Jesus (Phil. 2:5). Only in Scripture are we instructed in what that attitude is.

This is why the apostle Paul had emphasised to his young friend Timothy: 'Reflect on what I am saying, for the Lord will give you insight into all this' (2 Tim. 2:7). He was speaking about his own apostolic teaching in the letter he was writing. But his words apply to the whole of Scripture. Reflection on biblical teaching is our responsibility; insight is the wonderful gift which God will give to us through it.

Rebuking

Some Christians seem to use the Bible a great deal for rebuking—usually rebuking others! But that is not what Paul has in mind here. He is explaining to Timothy that it is through Scripture that God rebukes, or reproves us when we stand in need of his admonitions.

The Bible not only instructs our minds; it touches our consciences. The word 'rebukes' is the same word which describes the ministry of the Holy Spirit in John 16:8–11. He convicts, or convinces the world of sin, righteousness and judgment, in order to make men conscious of their need of Christ, and of Christ as the answer to their need. This is how the Bible is 'able to make you wise for salvation through faith in Christ Jesus' (2 Tim. 3:15).

It is a wonderful thing to be rebuked by God. We know that he does not do it for his own pleasure. He is not spiteful, but holy. We know too that his word is true, and for our good. Only as a last resort does he reprove us publicly. He prefers to work secretly and quietly, and he always works deeply and thoroughly. That is why it is such a privilege to have an open Bible and freedom to pray without molestation. We can expose ourselves to the gentle pain of a Divine Rebuker who is also the Divine Lover.

In our personal Bible study, and in the way we listen to the teaching of God's word, there should normally be at the back of our minds this question: Is there a word of rebuke for me in this passage of Scripture? Is God touching some sensitive (or desensitised) area of my conscience, in order to restore me to the kind of fellowship with him I once knew? So Charles Wesley taught the Methodists (and all the followers of the Lord) to pray:

> While now Thine oracles we read,
>   With earnest prayer and strong desire,
> O let Thy Spirit from Thee proceed,
>   Our souls to awaken and inspire,
> Our weakness help, our darkness chase,
> And guide us by the light of grace!
>
> Whene'er in error's paths we rove,
>   The living God through sin forsake,
> Our conscience by Thy Word reprove,
>   Convince and bring the wanderers back,
> Deep wounded by Thy Spirit's sword,
> And then by Gilead's balm restored.

Correcting

To most people the ideas conveyed by 'rebuke' and 'correct' are very similar. We often use the words as synonyms. But the expressions Paul uses convey different ideas.

We have noticed that 'rebuke' means convict, and is used in that sense elsewhere in the New Testament. But the word 'correct' is what students of grammar call a *hapax legomenon* ('a once-saider' as my classics master at school used to say): there is no other example of its use in the New Testament.

Paul's word is a most interesting one. It is used in the Greek version of the Old Testament Scriptures in the sense of repairing something which requires to be mended or rebuilt. It is the same Greek root from which we get our expressions 'orthodontics' (correcting irregularities in teeth), 'orthopaedics' (correcting or curing deformities in children). The Greek word is *orthos*, which means straight. So, when we speak of someone's 'orthodoxy' we mean that the views they hold (*doxa*, an opinion, view) are regular, or correct. Perhaps we would do well to remember the medical use when we think about Scripture making us 'orthodox'. It does not mean that we live lives which leave a nasty taste in people's mouths! Alas for us and them if we do. It means that our minds have been healed by God's truth, that our doctrine is 'sound', that is: *healthy* (1 Tim. 1:10; 2 Tim. 1:13; Titus 1:9, 13; 2:1, 2).

In other words, the value of Scripture is that it heals and cleanses our emotions and affections. It restores our broken lives to a condition of spiritual health and vitality. The Bible gets us into condition! That is why its fourth purpose is 'training'.

Training in Righteousness

In natural life we get ourselves into condition by exercise; we need to get into training.

It so happens that just at the time of writing this book I am trying (again!) to get into better physical condition. I have beside me Dr. Kenneth Cooper's famous book *Aerobics* ('Two million copies in print!' the cover tells me). I am trying my best to understand *why* my body needs exercise, and then I am carefully putting into practice the advice he gives. He tells me how healthy I will be—and warns me how unhealthy I probably am. He explains how much stronger my lungs, heart and nerves will be if I follow through the training programme. As I do so, and as he warned, I am finding just how out of condition I really am. While following the exercises I have found more perspiration and aches in the muscles than I expected! But the programme continues, and I stick to it. The exercise comes more easily, the 'pain barrier' seems to disappear. I begin to take the effort in my stride, and reach out for new barriers to overcome. Hopefully my whole being is benefiting! 'If you want to be healthy, *exercise*' is the motto.

Now, that is no less true in the life of the Spirit. The Spirit of God wants to get us 'into shape' spiritually. To be precise, he wants to get us into the shape that Christ was in. All God's commands say: be like Jesus! All God's work has this aim: to make us like Jesus. The word of God is the gymnasium in which we begin to get into true spiritual condition to enjoy a full Christian life. There is a hint of this in 1 Timothy 4:6–8. Paul tells his young friend that bodily exercise has some value, but spiritual exercise has lasting benefits. So, he says, 'train yourself to be godly'. The verb he uses has a familiar ring about it. It is *gumnazo*—'get into the gymnasium of the Bible' he is saying: 'get stripped for some action'. Invest in a training programme!

What a tremendous promise this is, and an encouragement to give ourselves to Bible study. Once we understand the blessing it will bring to us and the influences it will have on our character and manner of life, we should be enthusiastic about it. Should we not be ashamed when we see athletes at all levels who devote so much time and energy to get themselves into condition for perishing wreaths of glory? Let us get into training for the prize which is imperishable. And, says Paul to his young friend Timothy, 'Get into training in the word *now*, before you are out of condition spiritually, and lack the energy to begin!'

The purpose of God's word is to teach, rebuke, correct and train us in the way of life. But what of its effect?

The Effect of the Bible

A book was published a number of years ago containing messages from the famous Chinese Christian leader Ni To-sheng (Watchman Nee, as he was more popularly known). It bore the arresting title *The Normal Christian Worker*. In a word this is how Paul describes the effect of the study of the Bible. It makes men and women of God 'normal'. That is really what the words 'thoroughly equipped' mean.

The expression Paul uses comes from the word for completeness or normality, 'things as they should be'. The same root reappears in Mark 1:19, to describe the disciples mending or 'preparing' (N.I.V.) their nets—stitching the holes, cleaning and folding them for use on the next night. Again this root is used in Paul's statement that the ministries of the word which Christ has given to the Church have the great aim of preparing God's people for works of service (Eph. 4:12).

What Paul has in mind is this. We notice some Christians, and think to ourselves: What an outstanding example he is! He is just the kind of Christian I ought to be. But when we look at Jesus, we see that he alone is the only man who has ever been truly 'normal'. We are all, by comparison, abnormal. Yet God has a plan to bring us back to spiritual normality in Christ. He takes us, through the word he has given us (and the various ministries of it he has gifted to the Church), and like the disciples sitting by the shore of Galilee, he begins patiently to mend and restore our lives, until we are fit, 'thoroughly equipped', 'properly kitted out' for the service of his kingdom.

It cannot be too strongly emphasised that, while God

may work very radically and suddenly in our lives through all kinds of crises (and if he does so we must bow to his wisdom), that is not his greatest pleasure. His work is usually strongest in our lives when he has taken time to work deeply and thoroughly. That is how he works on us through Scripture.

I can think of no better vision to hold out before myself as I engage in the study of God's word than the story which shows God as the Refiner of his people:

A refiner of silver was observed patiently heating and refining the precious metal in front of him. After watching his patient work over a long period of time, the observer asked: 'How long will you work and patiently wait in order to refine this precious metal?' The refiner answered: 'Until I can see myself reflected in it.'

This should be our vision of what God is doing to us as we read and obey his word, so that our prayer will be: 'Work on, O Great Refiner, till the image of your Living Word is seen in me as I read your written word.'

> The sacred lessons of Thy grace,
>   Transmitted through Thy Word, repeat
> And train us up in all Thy ways
>   To make us in Thy will complete;
> Fulfil Thy love's redeeming plan,
> And bring us to a perfect man.
>
> Furnished out of Thy treasury,
>   O may we always ready stand
> To help the souls redeemed by Thee,
>   In what their various states demand;
> To teach, convince, correct, reprove,
> And build them up in holiest love!
>
> (Charles Wesley)

7   Seed Needs Soil

On one occasion Jesus issued a very significant word of warning to those who listened to his teaching and preaching. He said: 'Consider carefully how you listen' (Luke 8:18).

Many of us have strong instincts built into our Christian lives by a similar statement Jesus made. For he also warned us to be very careful about *what* we hear (Mark 4:24). These two different sayings are worth comparing. The second encourages us to exercise discernment in relation to the truth or falsehood of the teaching we are given. It charges us to examine what others are saying. But the first saying has a different role in the Christian's experience. It asks him to examine himself; to ask himself whether he is in tune with God and his will as he reveals himself through his word.

The preceding chapters have dealt with this question of carefully considering how we listen to God's word—for ourselves in personal Bible study, and for others whom we may teach. There are ways of studying the Bible which are, more than other ways, consistent with what the Bible is and the message it contains. Taking care *how* we hear obliges us to think through these problems. But there is, undoubtedly, another level at which we should examine what it means to listen to God's word. For reading the Bible is not merely an intellectual matter. How could it be when the Bible is a Spirit-inspired book intended to touch our lives with the presence of God? Is our aim to be changed and made more like Christ through our reading of God's word? Then we must also seek to develop those spiritual qualities in our own lives which enable us to hear God's voice with increasing clarity and to live in obedience to it.

Jesus told a parable to illustrate this point. In fact he told what could be called *the* parable in this context. Early in his ministry he indicated that those who hear God's word can be divided into a number of different categories of 'hearers'. He outlined the characteristics of each category and explained what it was in men's hearts and lives which put them in these categories.

Of the four different kinds of 'hearers' of God's word only one kind lastingly welcomes God's grace and perseveres in it—even when the preacher is the Lord Jesus Christ himself! That would have been a solemn enough thought had Jesus expressed it towards the end of his ministry when the multitudes had begun to drift away from him into the border regions of discipleship. But in fact our Lord's words, spoken so early in his ministry, clearly predicted that this was the way things would be.

Many Christians are better at taking heed to *what* they hear than they are at taking heed *how* they hear. But recognising false teaching is not at all the same thing, as obedient and fruitful listening to the truth. We very much need to ask ourselves where we stand in this matter. We can do this now with the help of our Lord's teaching in the parable of the sower and the soils. The question with which we are to be faced is: What kind of soil for the seed of God's word is your life?

When the Palestine farmer went out to sow his crops the scene was totally different from that surrounding the modern farmer in the western world. This farmer was not an expert in farm machinery, agricultural science, book-keeping and a thousand and one other things. He was a simple farmer. His machinery was a little bag, his mobility depended entirely on his own two feet! As he walked across the field he cast the seed down in strips. But he did know a little about practical economics. He knew that not all of his seed would find lodging in good soil. Some of it would fall on the path; some would undoubtedly fall on the shallow soil which lightly covered the limestone beneath—indeed he could see the limestone jutting out here and there; some would fall among the thorn seeds which would spring up and choke the wheat.

All this he knew. But he also knew that it was not practically possible to avoid this. If he were going to distribute the seed, then he knew that some of his seed—his good seed indeed—would never provide the crop he desired. His chief encouragement was that much seed might fall on good soil and produce a harvest, perhaps a ten-fold harvest, which would satisfy him.

Even as these thoughts passed through his mind, the farmer would see the birds swooping down on to the path to pick up the seed which fell there moments before. As he turned to go home—later to return with his little plough (since sowing preceded ploughing in Palestine)—perhaps he reflected that within a short time growth would begin to appear from the seeds which had fallen in the limestone soil. He would not even plough that soil. How different life would be if the good soil produced as quickly as the limestone soil! He would be able to do his economics on his fingers: 'If one seed produced a ten-fold fruit, and I were able to produce a crop at twice the present rate, what percentage increase would I find in my profits? What would the tax levy increase to? Would we be able to build a new house in five years?' Then he would return from his daydream. He knew from long experience how short-lived the seed sown on the limestone would be. It may have caused him to reflect on whether he could do anything about the thorny soil which would enable him to increase his profits. With these thoughts on his mind the ploughman turned for home.

Every one of Jesus' hearers that day was familiar with the situation he described. Many of them knew it from personal experience. Like listeners to sermons today, they probably went off at tangents in their minds from time to time, picturing their own fields, smiling in response to Jesus' description as they remembered an incident which tallied perfectly with what he was saying. Some of them probably returned home to share reminiscences of the 'old days', when they too had scattered the seed and ploughed the field. Some went away, doubtless, wondering just exactly what Jesus had been trying to say. There would be others who moved round the crowd as it dispersed, excitedly saying to their friends what an amazing fellow Jesus was, and what an incredible preacher! Some, too, seemed to live totally different lives when they came home—even the neighbours noticed. But it lasted for just a matter of months—until things began to change, and following Jesus became too demanding a way of life. Soon their enthusiasm began to wane. But there were some—indeed there proved to be many—who found that what Jesus had said began to change their whole lives. They could never be the same men and women again—and they never were!

There is no escaping the fact that one of the most crucial matters in the study of the Bible is the disposition, the spirit, the heart with which we come to read or hear it. The all-important question therefore becomes: What kind of hearer of God's word am I? What kind of soil in our Lord's parable best illustrates my life? Am I like the pathway, or the limestone soil, or perhaps like the thorn-ridden land? Or is my heart good soil for the Sower to plant the seed of the word of life?

The Pathway

The different kinds of soil in Jesus' parable are obviously intended to represent different kinds of hearers of God's word. But we discover that we fit into different categories at different times in our experience. It is not impossible for poor soil to be cleansed of its weeds, or for good soil to become weed-infested. The real issue is: What is my present state of heart as I approach the Bible message?

Some of us are like the pathway. God's word in our hearts is like the seed which lies on the firm surface of the well-trodden path. It is unlikely that it will ever be given the opportunity to penetrate in a manner that will create strong and enduring Christian character. Because of the hardness of the path it is easy for the birds to swoop down and to make off with the seed. So, in the life of the spirit, Jesus explains that the devil swoops down and steals the precious seed of the word away from men's minds, and it has no gracious effect on their lives. Martin Luther once said that while we cannot stop the birds flying around us, we ought to be able to prevent them from making their nests on our heads! If we realise that to be a child of God is also to be a soldier in a spiritual battle, we need to learn how to keep the devil at bay. We need to know what particular weaknesses destroy our defences against him. Jesus is our Teacher here, and puts his finger on two particular things.

Ignorance

The reason that the word of God can make so little impression on our lives may be that we do not understand it (Matt. 13:19). There may be times when we find things in the Bible which are difficult for us to understand: Simon Peter recognised this (2 Pet. 3:16). There are times when we may find it difficult to follow what is being said in a Bible study, or a sermon or talk. That could be the fault of the speaker rather than our fault! But Jesus is not speaking about this kind of failure to understand. The ignorance about which he speaks lies primarily in the heart, not in the intellect.

The parable which he told is an illustration of this. It does not take a high level of mental ability to understand it. Yet while the disciples were not all dunces, they confessed they could not understand it! Their failure was not lack of education, but lack of spiritual sensitivity and under-standing. The New Testament calls this a sclerosis of the heart (*sklērocardia*, Mark 10:5; 16:14), a hardness of heart which produces a disinterest in, and an inability to under-stand the message of the gospel.

This was a major characteristic of Paul's earlier life. God had mercy on him, even although he had persecuted the Church, because he had done so in gross ignorance (1 Tim. 1:13). He was familiar with the message of the Bible. His knowledge of its contents went far beyond the ordinary Jew of his day. Yet there was a kind of veil on his heart whenever he read the Old Testament (cf. 2 Cor. 3:15). He did not understand that it pointed men to their sinfulness and their need for someone to be their Saviour! Only through the working of the Holy Spirit in his heart (Rom. 7:7–13) did he eventually discover the truth about himself, about God, and about Christ. His story could be multiplied in countless instances.

This sclerosis of the heart is a condition from which none of us is permanently immune. The biographies of the great Christians down through the centuries witness to the fact that the more we grow in grace the more we may become conscious that there still remains a path-like quality to the way we read and hear God's word.

Today, as we read a section from God's word, and tomorrow, when we listen to the teaching of it, it may bear little fruit because our hearts have grown cold and hard. We are not allowing it the room it needs to work in a life-transforming way. We need to come to God in prayer, confess our need, thank him that he has begun to make us conscious of it, and ask him to enable us to respond more gladly and fully to what we read and hear. It is surely one of the greatest mistakes we can make to assume that our own hearts are permanently in a condition before God which makes them suitable soil for the seed of his word. Our lamentable spiritual powerlessness gives the lie to that assumption. We stand in need of his grace *always* when we turn to his word.

Worldliness

Here is the second thing to which Jesus refers. Why is the pathway such an unwelcoming receptacle for the seed? Because as the seed lies on the path, foot after foot tramples it down. The problem, in part, is that it is destroyed by the traffic of the everyday world which passes over it; 'it was trampled on' (Luke 8:5) says Jesus.

Is it reading too much into these words to compare the path with the condition of many people's hearts? The ordinary, legitimate pressures of the society in which we live, with its hustle and bustle, can so easily press the word of God nearer and nearer to the perimeter of our concerns, until its influence is almost totally eradicated.

There are some people for whom the feet which trample across the ground are those belonging to the day-to-day world of Christian activity. How many of us, for example, are so busy in Christian work that the word of God has been relegated to a corner in our routine? We would never dream of calling that 'worldliness', but that is exactly what it is. Paradoxically, doing nothing but reading the Bible may also be worldliness, rooted in a refusal to conform our lives to the teaching of Scripture which constantly sends us from reading our Bible to being salt and light in society! Worldliness is a chameleon in the heart, and it can disguise itself against many backgrounds.

But what is worldliness, really? It is, of course, conforming the way we think and live to the norms of this world, rather than the norms of the world in which God lives. It is making something other than the Bible the rule of our lives. It is developing a life-style which has fundamentally different principles to the life-style of a disciple of Jesus. The result is that when we come to read the Bible we are out of harmony with it. We bring our own preconceived ideas to it, and we are unable to hear what it is really saying to us.

When we come to read the Bible, therefore, we must confess all this to God in a humble spirit and with a serious intention. He has promised to turn our hearts of stone into hearts of flesh.

The rocky soil

At first glance, the rocky soil might be thought by city-dwellers to represent the hypocritical heart—it promises much (early growth) but in the end produces little. But our Lord's words refer less to hypocrisy and more to super-ficiality. It is not so much a matter of deliberate deception as a matter of shallowness of reception. Simon Kistemaker accurately describes the scene:

At first it appears that the seed sown on rocky places gets an early start. The summer heat, captured in the rock substratum below, is now gradually released in the months of November and December. There is sufficient rainfall, so that the necessary warmth and moisture make early germination possible. These green shoots spring up quickly, and while the rest of the field is still barren, they make quite an impressive show. The trained eye of the farmer sees the difference. He knows that the appearance of the green stalks of grain on the rocky places is decep-tive; when the rains have ceased, and the sun in the spring of the year rises with increasing heat, the plants wither. They have no roots that go deep down into the soil to supply the plants with water. The plants shrivel up and die.

(*The Parables of Jesus* p26)

'They have no roots that go deep down into the soil.' The untrained, inexperienced observer may not notice, but the trained eye of the farmer does. He is not so easily impressed. Long experience has made him wary of such startling results!

What is the parallel to this in the response we make to God's word? Our Lord's interpretation of his own parable (given in Matt. 13:18–23; Luke 8:11–15; Mark 4:13–20) appears to underline two characteristics of the heart which sometimes produce startling responses to God's word.

An untested response

We receive the word 'with joy'. The response is instantaneous, and the sense of happiness is immediate. What is wrong with that? The answer must surely be, nothing whatsoever! We would be spiritual Scrooges if we thought otherwise. Christ came to bring light and life, joy and peace to our lives. We should rejoice that the Gospel makes men joyful! Moreover, there is plenty of evidence in the New Testament to show that this is exactly what it did. Jesus told his disciples that the production of his joy in their lives was one of the great purposes of his ministry to them (John 15:11). Joy was a characteristic response to the preaching of the word in the early years of the Church (Acts 8:8; 1 Thess. 1:6).

But our Lord's salutary word is that immediate growth may be deceptive, and it may well prove to be temporary. The tell-tale sign is when joy and gladness constitute the whole of the response to God's word. We may contrast the experience of the Thessalonians: 'in spite of severe suffering, you welcomed the message with the joy given by the Holy Spirit' (1 Thess. 1:6). This was the reason that Paul could be so confident, that God himself had chosen them (1 Thess. 1:4). Their response had already been tested in the fires of affliction and persecution.

This is not to say that an immediate response, or a joyful response will necessarily prove to be a spurious one. But if that is all there is to it, then the new plant is in grave danger. The same is true in the world of nature: if we plant seed and it flowers with miraculous speed, we ought to exercise caution about its longevity. The plant will need to face more severe testing before it has the strength to last. So much depends on the depth and strength of the roots. So, says Jesus, when someone who has responded in this way suddenly meets persecution or affliction, his lack of a deep work of grace will begin to show. The hot blast of opposition may cause him to shrivel and die. Trials and difficulties in the Christian life invariably have this effect. They kill enthusiasm which is rootless and therefore graceless; but they strengthen the graces of the Spirit which have begun to send down strong and lasting roots into the love of God.

Concentration on the short-term

The modern mania for quick results is one from which Christians are not immune. How short-sighted we are, and how often our lives revolve around the immediate rather than the long-term! But the effect of God's word is intended to be long-term. We have a God who intends to take his time in our lives and to work deeply and thoroughly. In fact, God is much more interested in how deeply the roots of grace go down into our character than he is with the spectacular impressions of short-term enthusiasm for his kingdom.

What difference does this make to the way in which we approach God's word? It means that our study will only begin to produce the desired effect so long as we are willing to labour patiently in coming to understand it and put it into practical application in daily experience. We need to strengthen and develop Christian graces over a period of time. This is why there is such an emphasis in the New Testament on being properly rooted (Col. 2:6–7; Eph. 3:17–19; John 15:4–5, 7–8).

There is no short cut. There is no substitute for the dedicated labour of becoming thoroughly acquainted with God's mind and will as he has opened them to us in the Bible. Nor does the New Testament see any substitute in life for those difficulties which will put our spiritual development to the test, destroying what is unreal and strengthening what is true. It is through hardships that we enter the kingdom of God (Acts 14:22). If there is to be lasting fruit, then there must be divine pruning (John 15:2).

This should be a warning to some of us and an encouragement to others. For spiritual life is not to be measured exclusively along the scale of apparent development. It should often be measured in terms of the amount of opposition which it has to overcome to survive. It takes greater pressure to withstand the force of a twenty-stone man than it does to overthrow a light-weight boy! Success in the Christian life is to be measured similarly—not necessarily by the degree of joy experienced, but by its quality. For joy in tribulation (Rom. 5:3) is true growth, and a balanced response to the grace of God in the Gospel. This was the confession of the author of Psalm 119:

> Your word is a lamp to my feet
>   and a light to my path.
> I have taken an oath and confirmed it,
>   that I will follow your righteous laws.
> I have suffered much;
>   renew my life, O Lord, according to your word.
> Accept, O Lord, the willing praise of my mouth,
>   and teach me your laws.

Though I constantly take my life in my hands,
   I will not forget your law.
The wicked have set a snare for me,
   but I have not strayed from your precepts.
Your statutes are my heritage forever;
   they are the joy of my heart.
My heart is set on keeping your decrees
   to the very end.

                                    (Psalm 119:105–112)

It is when obedience to the Lord's word becomes more important to us than the experience of joy that roots have begun to undergird our lives.

The thorny soil

The first two categories which Jesus described involved short-term responses to God's word. In the case of the pathway, the rejection was virtually immediate; in the case of the rocky soil, a little slower. But this kind of response involves the passage of time before its true nature becomes evident. There appears to be genuine growth. There may even be a measure of resistance to opposition, trials and persecution.

But we would be poor students of human nature and of Scripture if we assumed that there were only two ways to destroy the seed of God's word when it is sown. It would be a great mistake to think that the devil disappears from the scene when he has stolen the seed from the 'pathway' hearer! On the contrary, he has a hand in the spurious joy of the rocky soil too. What is more significant is that, if he fails here, he has other avenues of approach.

Many a Christian who has remained unspoiled by the rigours of trials has been caught in the net of ease and plenty. King David is an example (2 Sam. 11:1ff), and King

Uzziah another (2 Chron. 26:15, 16). We may be able to exercise true mastery of our situation more easily when we are in need than when we abound, and never learn the secret of facing both without being turned away from God's word by our sin (Phil. 4:12, 13). So Jesus warns us that it is possible to have a thorny heart—one that becomes swamped by the cares and interests of this world. The anxieties of having and the anxieties of not having can equally deal mortal blows to the life of the professing Christian.

What has happened in such a person's life? They have neglected the necessary work of weeding. When the seed has been sown in the heart, it has been allowed to lodge there without any effort being made to deal with desires, ambitions and personal failings. These, if given a chance, will develop and eventually choke what has been accomplished by the word. The subtle element in all this is that under such circumstances we are inclined to wonder what we did wrong. The answer, as far as we can see, is nothing. And that is precisely what is wrong—we did nothing. We did not weed out what was alien to Christ. Consequently we pay the penalty, as our hearts are taken up with a multitude of other things, and God's word is neglected.

This has unusual relevance to our spiritual climate today. We live in a period when Christians, conscious of the Victorian image which they have in society at large, are concerned to be much more positive in their whole approach to life. No longer do we want to say that a Christian is a person who 'doesn't do' one thing or another. We want to express much more positively the life of Christ in the Church.

There is something very natural and healthy about this. But not when we develop an unbiblical and unbalanced emphasis which neglects everything Scripture has to say to us negatively. If we are to develop the great positive graces of the Spirit in our lives, it will be at the expense of ridding ourselves of the evils in our hearts. In order to say 'yes' to all that Christ has given us, we need to do a great deal of weeding out of everything which stands against his word and will. Neglect here will mean greater troubles later. The subtle feature we need to reckon with is that the evil does not need to be planted—it is already there, and will inevitably make its presence felt. The onus is on us to make sure that it receives no opportunity to do so.

Three kinds of soils: the pathway type, the rocky type, the thorn-ridden type. Each one illustrates that there is a special relationship between our reading and hearing of God's word and the moral and spiritual condition of our lives. It is against this background that Jesus invites us to ask and answer the question each time we open the Bible to read and study it: What kind of soil am I?

The good soil

How can we be good soil for the word of God? How can we hear, receive and produce fruit?

It is obvious from the rest of the parable what will be necessary.

Ploughing will be needed, to create an honest and good heart for God's word. Jeremiah-like, we will have to hear the word which calls for a breaking up of the ground which has never truly been ploughed (Jer. 4:3). That means we will first of all become deeply conscious of our sclerosed hearts, and ask God to make them fresh and tender in his hands.

Rooting will be needed, in order that we may 'keep' or 'retain' (Luke 8:15) the word. We need to make obedience to God's word a matter of conscience: not treating it in a take-it-or-leave-it fashion, but reading God's word as in his presence, speaking to him about our needs and failures in the light of his truth, and with a serious intention seeing disobedience to his commands as sin.

Weeding will be needed. What a comfort it is that Jesus speaks about 'by persevering producing a crop' (Luke 8:15). 'Stickability' is itself a great grace. We must keep going on, trusting that God will keep his promise to use his word to change us, gradually, into the image of his Son Jesus Christ.

He who has ears to hear, let him hear.

8   Speaking Personally

'How do you actually go about it?' That is always the question which is asked. 'How can I study the Bible so that I will get maximum benefit from it, and find that it really helps me to grow in my spiritual experience and in the knowledge of God?'

I want, in the last few pages of our study together, to share some practical advice, based largely on personal experience and observation. Personally I have always found other Christians' comments on Bible study to be both interesting and helpful. Sometimes we are stimulated by their abilities, at other times we learn from their mistakes. It is a good thing to compare notes in every area of life. This chapter is simply a comparing of notes. It may be that you will find more value in doing Bible study in a very different way from any of these I would suggest. The important thing is that you should begin to think through your own method of Bible study, and find a way of doing it which is spiritually helpful.

Discipline

We have already noticed in passing the first prerequisite to real Bible study. Paul told Timothy that he needed to work hard at it (2 Tim. 2:15). There must be discipline. Otherwise our study of God's word will be crowded out of our lives, and become an 'extra' rather than a necessity. We must make Bible study a priority. That may not be easy; indeed, at few times in our lives will it be easy. It is not any easier for the housewife than it is for the husband who works from nine to five. It is usually easier when we are young, and have fewer responsibilities consuming our time. But even then, we have to 'make' time. In biblical language we have to 'redeem' time. We have to purchase it by sacrificing some other use to which we might have devoted it. You and I will never make any real progress until this becomes a settled principle in our thinking.

What does this mean in practice? It is important to say that we must not get ourselves into a sense of unhealthy bondage about this. The most important thing is that we get to know our Bibles, *however we do it*. It is not necessarily more profitable to study the Bible at 5 a.m. than at 5 p.m.! There is nothing necessarily spiritual about any hour of the day, early or late. But there are very obvious advantages in doing our study at a regular hour, where that is possible. Most of us need routines of this sort if we are to carry through a long-term project. One only needs to read the training manuals to see that this is by no means an exclusively spiritual principle. It is, again for most of us, the best way to get the maximum out of life, and to put the maximum into it.

Robert Murray M'Cheyne used to try to set aside his best hours of the day for study. Perhaps we can learn something from that. But some of us are already committed, usually to our daily work, during our best hours. Can we perhaps use time that tends to be given over to nothing very much? Do we have some time before work, or could we make time then? Is there time when the dishes have been washed after the evening meal? What about time during the lunch-break? Those who do jobs which isolate them from others at that time of day may find Bible study, done sandwich in hand, a great pleasure. What about that half hour you tend to waste watching television? The programme you did want to see is finished, the next one is only of marginal interest. Yet night after night you watch extra programmes. Why not turn off and get out the Bible?

We are all different. Our families and our routines are different. There are no laws which apply to every circumstance—only one necessity: make sure that you give regular time to study God's word.

What about a method?

There are many Bible study aids available today. Many people use the Scripture Union Bible Reading notes, which provide some comment for each day, and will guide you through the whole Bible over a period of several years. A manual much used by students is called *Search the Scriptures* (Inter-Varsity), and takes the reader through the entire Bible in a period of three years, reading roughly one chapter each day. Questions are supplied to encourage careful thought, and many people, not necessarily students, may find this enormously helpful.

Whatever notes or methods you may use, try to consider the following points.

First, read the entire Bible. It is possible, without too much strain, to read the entire Bible during the course of one year. You will find such a course of reading printed as an appendix to this book, and you may find it helpful to use it. It involves reading only three chapters each day of the year. If it is followed year after year, it will not be long before you are very familiar with the whole of the Bible.

Secondly, read whole books of the Bible at a sitting. There is nothing like reading a Letter or a Gospel in this way—as though you had never read it before. You will find things come home to you by reading right through—insights which had never crossed your mind before. Often it is helpful to read in a different translation from the one you usually use.

I will never forget, as a teenager, spending my entire

pocket money on a paperback edition of J. B. Phillips' new translation of the Book of Revelation. I had to walk home from town, having spent all my money! But I can still sense the tremendous excitement which gripped me as I snuggled in a chair beside the fire. That afternoon I began to understand for the very first time what the Book of Revelation was about. I felt that I could see it all before my mind's eye; as though I were there, watching the triumph and victory of Christ come to pass. I had a glimpse, however small, of what that book has meant to beleaguered Christians down through the ages. I began to see with fresh eyes that the Lord God omnipotent reigns!

Such experiences will probably be rare. They will often be associated with special needs in our own lives. But nevertheless we will always benefit from reading in this way. It was the way that the New Testament Letters, for example, were first read, and it enables us to catch the great force of their teaching.

Thirdly, recognise that some books are more significant than others. There is a sense in which some books of the Bible are more important than others, although they are all equally inspired by God. He has given these books in a very definite arrangement. Some of them more clearly present the message of the gospel than others do. Some stress more central themes than others. It therefore makes a good deal of sense to try to grapple with the message of the central books of Scripture at greater depth, so that in turn we will have fresh insight into the meaning of all the others. It may therefore prove to be a marvellous investment of time to spend a year, or some longer period of time, getting the message of one book more clearly understood. Books like Genesis, Psalms, Isaiah, John's Gospel, Acts, Romans, Galatians and Hebrews lend themselves to this kind of study. Speaking personally, I remain deeply grateful to God that it dawned on me at a time in my life when it was possible to devote time to serious study, that such books as these, when rightly understood, take one into the very heart and mind of God himself.

There are many tools for the job. It is always helpful, besides a good translation (like *The New International Version*) to have a concordance, which will help you to find cross-references, and some kind of Bible Dictionary, to explain many of the background features to the books of the Bible. There are also a number of helpful one-volume Bible Commentaries available. I have personally found *The New Bible Commentary Revised* to be helpful. The *Wycliffe Bible Commentary* is also extremely valuable as well as being modern. Older commentaries which are helpful (and usually more devotional in style) include those by Jamieson, Faussett and Brown; Matthew Henry (available in an abridged form) and Matthew Poole. A minister or Christian bookseller will be able to recommend many more, particularly individual commentaries (for in-depth study).

You may find it helpful to take some notes. It will certainly be vital to take time to pray about what has been learned from God's word. Prayer makes the soil of the heart fertile for the seed of the word of God. It is the way to overcome those periods of dryness which all of us who study the Bible experience from time to time. Christians we may be, but we still need the constant help of the Holy Spirit if we are to feel the power of God's word. We need to pray that he will always come to open our eyes, so that we find nuggets of valuable truth, pieces of real, practical wisdom, warning and advice about our lives, in the Scriptures we read.

The Bible is a great book. It is *the* Book. But it does need to be handled with care. If we do so handle it, then we will discover what the Psalmist meant when he said:

Oh, how I love your law!
    I meditate on it all day long.
Your commands make me wiser than my enemies,
    for they are ever with me.

I have more insight than all my teachers,
    for I meditate on your statutes.
I have more understanding than the elders,
    for I obey your precepts.
I have kept my feet from every evil path
    so that I might obey your word.
I have not departed from your laws,
    for you yourself have taught me.
How sweet are your promises to my taste,
    sweeter than honey to my mouth!
I gain understanding from your precepts;
    therefore I hate every wrong path.
Your word is a lamp to my feet
    and a light to my path.

Bible Reading Plan

The following plan for Bible reading will take you through the entire Bible during the course of a year. It requires the reading of three chapters each day. The plan suggests these should be read in the morning, at midday and then in the evening. It may be more suitable for you to find a different schedule, for example: morning, after the evening meal and at bed time.

JANUARY

	Morning Genesis	Midday Matthew	Evening Ezra
1	1	1	1
2	2	2	2
3	3	3	3
4	4	4	4
5	5	5	5
6	6	6	6
7	7	7	7
8	8	8	8
9	9, 10	9	9
10	11	10	10
11	12	11	Nehemiah 1
12	13	12	2
13	14	13	3
14	15	14	4
15	16	15	5
16	17	16	6
17	18	17	7
18	19	18	8
19	20	19	9
20	21	20	10
21	22	21	11
22	23	22	12
23	24	23	13
24	25	24	Esther 1
25	26	25	2
26	27	26	3
27	28	27	4
28	29	28	5
29	30	Mark 1	6
30	31	2	7
31	32	3	8

FEBRUARY

	Morning Genesis	Midday Mark	Evening Esther / Job
1	33	4	Esther 9, 10
2	34	5	Job 1
3	35, 36	6	2
4	37	7	3
5	38	8	4
6	39	9	5
7	40	10	6
8	41	11	7
9	42	12	8
10	43	13	9
11	44	14	10
12	45	15	11
13	46	16	12
14	47	Luke 1–v 38	13
15	48	1 v 39	14
16	49	2	15
17	50	3	16, 17
18	Exodus 1	4	18
19	2	5	19
20	3	6	20
21	4	7	21
22	5	8	22
23	6	9	23
24	7	10	24
25	8	11	25, 26
26	9	12	27
27	10	13	28
28	11, 12–v 21	14	29

MARCH

Day	Morning Exod	Midday Luke	Evening Job
1	12 v 22	15	30
2	13	16	31
3	14	17	32
4	15	18	33
5	16	19	34
6	17	20	35
7	18	21	36
8	19	22	37
9	20	23	38
10	21	24	39
11	22	John 1	40
12	23	2	41
13	24	3	42
14	25	4	Proverbs 1
15	26	5	2
16	27	6	3
17	28	7	4
18	29	8	5
19	30	9	6
20	31	10	7
21	32	11	8
22	33	12	9
23	34	13	10
24	35	14	11
25	36	15	12
26	37	16	13
27	38	17	14
28	39	18	15
29	40	19	16
30	Leviticus 1	20	17
31	2, 3	21	18

APRIL

Day	Morning Leviticus	Midday Psalms	Evening Proverbs
1	4	1, 2	19
2	5	3, 4	20
3	6	5, 6	21
4	7	7, 8	22
5	8	9	23
6	9	10	24
7	10	11, 12	25
8	11, 12	13, 14	26
9	13	15, 16	27
10	14	17	28
11	15	18	29
12	16	19	30
13	17	20, 21	31
14	18	22	Eccles 1
15	19	23, 24	2
16	20	25	3
17	21	26, 27	4
18	22	28, 29	5
19	23	30	6
20	24	31	7
21	25	32	8
22	26	33	9
23	27	34	10
24	Numbers 1	35	11
25	2	36	12
26	3	37	Song 1
27	4	38	2
28	5	39	3
29	6	40, 41	4
30	7	42, 43	5

MAY

	Morning	Midday	Evening
	Numbers	*Psalms*	*Song*
1	8	44	6
2	9	45	7
3	10	46, 47	8
4	11	48	*Isaiah* 1
5	12, 13	49	2
6	14	50	3, 4
7	15	51	5
8	16	52–54	6
9	17, 18	55	7
10	19	56, 57	8, 9–v 7
11	20	58, 59	9 v 8, 10 v 4
12	21	60, 61	10 v 5
13	22	62, 63	11, 12
14	23	64, 65	13
15	24	66, 67	14
16	25	68	15
17	26	69	16
18	27	70, 71	17, 18
19	28	72	19, 20
20	29	73	21
21	30	74	22
22	31	75, 76	23
23	32	77	24
24	33	78–v 37	25
25	34	78 v 38	26
26	35	79	27
27	36	80	28
28	*Deut* 1	81, 82	29
29	2	83, 84	30
30	3	85	31
31	4	86, 87	32

JUNE

	Morning	Midday	Evening
	Deut	*Psalms*	*Isaiah*
1	5	88	33
2	6	89	34
3	7	90	35
4	8	91	36
5	9	92, 93	37
6	10	94	38
7	11	95, 96	39
8	12	97, 98	40
9	13, 14	99–101	41
10	15	102	42
11	16	103	43
12	17	104	44
13	18	105	45
14	19	106	46
15	20	107	47
16	21	108, 109	48
17	22	110, 111	49
18	23	112, 113	50
19	24	114, 115	51
20	25	116	52
21	26	117, 118	53
22	27, 28–v 19	119–v 24	54
23	28 v 20	v 25–48	55
24	29	v 49–72	56
25	30	v 73–96	57
26	31	v 97–120	58
27	32	v 121–144	59
28	33, 34	v 145–176	60
29	*Joshua* 1	120–122	61
30	2	123–125	62

JULY

Day	Morning	Midday (Ps)	Evening
1	Joshua 3	126–128	Isaiah 63
2	4	129–131	64
3	5, 6–v. 5	132–134	65
4	6 v. 6	135, 136	66
5	7	137, 138	Jeremiah 1
6	8	139	2
7	9	140, 141	3
8	10	142, 143	4
9	11	144	5
10	12, 13	145	6
11	14, 15	146, 147	7
12	16, 17	148	8
13	18, 19	149, 150	9
14	20, 21	Acts 1	10
15	22	2	11
16	23	3	12
17	24	4	13
18	Judges 1	5	14
19	2	6	15
20	3	7	16
21	4	8	17
22	5	9	18
23	6	10	19
24	7	11	20
25	8	12	21
26	9	13	22
27	10, 11–v. 11	14	23
28	11 v. 12	15	24
29	12	16	25
30	13	17	26
31	14	18	27

AUGUST

Day	Morning	Midday	Evening
1	Judges 15	Acts 19	Jeremiah 28
2	16	20	29
3	17	21	30, 31
4	18	22	32
5	19	23	33
6	20	24	34
7	21	25	35
8	Ruth 1	26	36, 45
9	2	27	37
10	3, 4	28	38
11	1 Samuel 1	Romans 1	39
12	2	2	40
13	3	3	41
14	4	4	42
15	5, 6	5	43
16	7, 8	6	44
17	9	7	46
18	10	8	47
19	11	9	48
20	12	10	49
21	13	11	50
22	14	12	51
23	15	13	52
24	16	14	Lament 1
25	17	15	2
26	18	16	3
27	19	1 Cor 1	4
28	20	2	5
29	21, 22	3	Ezekiel 1
30	23	4	2
31	24	5	3

SEPTEMBER

	Morning 1 Samuel	Midday 1 Cor	Evening Ezekiel
1	25	6	4
2	26	7	5
3	27	8	6
4	28	9	7
5	29, 30	10	8
6	31	11	9
7	2 Samuel 1	12	10
8	2	13	11
9	3	14	12
10	4, 5	15	13
11	6	16	14
12	7	2 Cor 1	15
13	8, 9	2	16
14	10	3	17
15	11	4	18
16	12	5	19
17	13	6	20
18	14	7	21
19	15	8	22
20	16	9	23
21	17	10	24
22	18	11	25
23	19	12	26
24	20	13	27
25	21	Galatians 1	28
26	22	2	29
27	23	3	30
28	24	4	31
29	1 Kings 1	5	32
30	2	6	33

OCTOBER

	Morning 1 Kings	Midday Ephesians	Evening Ezekiel
1	3	1	34
2	4, 5	2	35
3	6	3	36
4	7	4	37
5	8	5	38
6	9	6	39
7	10	Phil 1	40
8	11	2	41
9	12	3	42
10	13	4	43
11	14	Coloss 1	44
12	15	2	45
13	16	3	46
14	17	4	47
15	18	1 Thess 1	48
16	19	2	Daniel 1
17	20	3	2
18	21	4	3
19	22	5	4
20	2 Kings 1	2 Thess 1	5
21	2	2	6
22	3	3	7
23	4	1 Timothy 1	8
24	5	2	9
25	6	3	10
26	7	4	11
27	8	5	12
28	9	6	Hosea 1
29	10	2 Timothy 1	2
30	11, 12	2	3, 4
31	13	3	5, 6

NOVEMBER

Day	Morning	Midday	Evening
1	2 Kings 14	2 Timothy 4	Hosea 7
2	15	Titus 1	8
3	16	2	9
4	17	3	10
5	18	Philemon 1	11
6	19	Hebrews 1	12
7	20	2	13
8	21	3	14
9	22	4	Joel 1
10	23	5	2
11	24	6	3
12	25	7	Amos 1
13	1 Chr 1, 2	8	2
14	3, 4	9	3
15	5, 6	10	4
16	7, 8	11	5
17	9, 10	12	6
18	11, 12	13	7
19	13, 14	James 1	8
20	15	2	9
21	16	3	Obadiah 1
22	17	4	Jonah 1
23	18	5	2
24	19, 20	1 Peter 1	3
25	21	2	4
26	22	3	Micah 1
27	23	4	2
28	24, 25	5	3
29	26, 27	2 Peter 1	4
30	28	2	5

DECEMBER

Day	Morning	Midday	Evening
1	1 Chr 29	2 Peter 3	Micah 6
2	2 Chr 1	1 John 1	7
3	2	2	Nahum 1
4	3, 4	3	2
5	5, 6 – v 11	4	3
6	6 v 12	5	Habakkuk 1
7	7	2 John 1	2
8	8	3 John 1	3
9	9	Jude 1	Zephaniah 1
10	10	Rev 1	2
11	11, 12	2	3
12	13	3	Haggai 1
13	14, 15	4	2
14	16	5	Zechariah 1
15	17	6	2
16	18	7	3
17	19, 20	8	4
18	21	9	5
19	22, 23	10	6
20	24	11	7
21	25	12	8
22	26	13	9
23	27, 28	14	10
24	29	15	11
25	30	16	12, 13 – v 1
26	31	17	13 v 2
27	32	18	14
28	33	19	Malachi 1
29	34	20	2
30	35	21	3
31	36	22	4